IMPORTANT BILLING AND CREDIT REQUIREMENTS

All producers of DANCERS *must* give credit to the Author of the Play in all programs distributed in connection with performances of the Play and in all instances in which the title of the Play appears for purposes of advertising, publicizing or otherwise exploiting the Play and/or a production. The name of the Author *must* also appear on a separate line, in which no other name appears, immediately following the title, and *must* appear in size of type not less than fifty percent the size of the title type.

For My Family

DANCERS

by

MICHAEL GRADY

Best New Play,
1986 American College Theatre Festival

SAMUEL FRENCH, INC.
45 West 25th Street NEW YORK 10010
7623 Sunset Boulevard HOLLYWOOD 90046
LONDON TORONTO

ISBN 0 573 69042 1 Printed in U.S.A.

DANCERS premiered Sept. 18, 1985 at The University of Arizona's Park Theatre, with the following cast:

MONTCRIEF .... Arlene Toohey

KEVIN .... Stephen Yates

ORDERLY .... David Evans

JULIA.............................. Nancy Howard

NURSE .... Julie Volk

SUTTON .... Elise C. Wagner

JACK .... Christopher Wilken

RAYMOND .... Elaine Rewolinski

The Director was Rhonda Tinsley, the Stage Manager was Susan Pope, Set by Sharmin Pool, Lights by Joel Young, Costumes by Linda Dutra, and Sound and Technical Direction by Stephen Spoonamore, Props by Laura Kopec, and Assistant Direction by Michael Grady.

DANCERS played April 2-3 at The Kennedy Center in Washington, D.C., as part of The American College Theatre Festival. In its Washington version, the character of the Nurse was dropped, and Andy Davids took over the role of the Orderly. Laura Kopec stage-managed.

SYNOPSIS OF SCENES

ACT I

Scene 1: The solarium (Sun Room) of a large Michigan Nursing Home, night.

Scene 2: Julia's Room in the Nursing Home, several days later.

Scene 3: The Same, a few weeks later.

ACT II

Scene 1: The Solarium, a few minutes later.

Scene 2: Julia's Room, immediately afterward.

Scene 3: Solarium, the next day.

Scene 4: Julia's Room *and* the Solarium, later that day.

Scene 5: The Solarium, that night.

Scene 6: Julia's Room, the next day.

TIME: The Present

DANCERS

ACT ONE
SCENE ONE

The Solarium, night. We see a somewhat gloomy and harshly-lit room; old and dirty walls contrast with the metal-framed, vinyl-cushioned "waiting room" chair and sofa — on SR and SL respectively. Beside the chair is a small table and lamp, two ominous-looking swinging doors sit UR, downstage from the doors hangs a large bulletin board with a few tattered notices tacked to it. The sofa has two endtables with ashtrays, and DS we see an old radiator, a rack full of magazines, and some loose magazines strewn around the rack. A large "window" sits directly above the radiator in "the fourth wall." Plants have been placed here and there about the room, and a lightswitch sits directly adjacent to the swinging doors.

Enter MONTCRIEF, a nurse, with KEVIN behind her.

MONTCRIEF. Why don't you make yourself comfortable in here for awhile?

KEVIN. When will I be able to see her?

MONTCRIEF. The doctor is looking at her now.

KEVIN. But—

MONTCRIEF. We'll let you know, Mr. Birne, as soon as we can.

KEVIN. You'll be transferring her to the hospital, then?

MONTCRIEF. That may not be necessary. *(KEVIN makes to speak.)* We're not sure its a stroke. Those were her words—

KEVIN. Well, she would know, wouldn't she? It's her stroke.

MONTCRIEF. Your mother has a tendency to exaggerate, Mr. Birne. *(Pause.)* The doctor is looking at her now. If we have to move her from the nursing home to the hospital, we will—

KEVIN. Shouldn't you—?

MONTCRIEF. *If* it is a stroke. You'll know as soon as we know.

KEVIN. And when will that be?

MONTCRIEF and KEVIN. *(Together.)* The doctor is looking at her now.

MONTCRIEF. Would you mind waiting here in the meantime?

KEVIN. I was thinking of going to the cafeteria to wait.

MONTCRIEF. I'm afraid it's closed this time of night.

KEVIN. And the porch area?

MONTCRIEF. We lock that up at dusk.

KEVIN. I couldn't just stand in the hallway? *(She shakes her head.)* No, I wouldn't mind waiting here.

MONTCRIEF. We'll let you know if anything happens.

KEVIN. Thank you. I'll be here. *(She exits.)* ... in this ... lovely room. *(He walks around a bit.)* It could be nothing. *(Checks his watch.)* Just relax. *(He blinks at the harsh overhead lights, turns them off. Moonlight from the window illuminates the room.)* ...just relax *(He closes his eyes.)*

MONTCRIEF'S VOICE. *(from outside)* Could you come here a minute?

(KEVIN, by reflex, starts for the door. The voices of MONTCRIEF and the ORDERLY are heard from offstage, or they can be seen if a hallway unit is available.)

ORDERLY. I have to clean up 408. Mrs. LaRue knocked over her tray. *(KEVIN stops at the door, wanders back around the room.)*

MONTCRIEF. Wait a minute. *(KEVIN starts back for the door.)* Jeff? *(KEVIN stops again.)* Have you seen Mrs. Muir?

ORDERLY. Nope.

MONTCRIEF. I just checked 412, and she's not in her room.

(Sound of footsteps approaching.)

ORDERLY. She's probably in the Solarium. *(KEVIN turns, the ORDERLY comes in. They look at each other. Pause.)*

KEVIN. Hi.

MONTCRIEF. *(still offstage)* Is she in there?

ORDERLY. *(closing the door)* No, just this big guy. *(KEVIN sits.)*

MONTCRIEF. If you see Mrs. Muir—

ORDERLY. I won't see her unless she's under Mrs. LaRue's tray—

MONTCRIEF. She's supposed to be in bed. She shouldn't

be up this late.

ORDERLY. Can I go now? Mrs. LaRue is soaking in beef gravy. *(KEVIN crosses to the door, opens it, and makes to speak.)*

MONTCRIEF. You're awful cranky tonight.

ORDERLY. Well, maybe I have reason to be cranky—

MONTCRIEF. *(a whisper)* Well, maybe this isn't the place to talk about it. *(KEVIN decides better of speaking, goes back into the room, sits.)*

(Enter MONTCRIEF.)

MONTCRIEF. Mr. Birne? *(He stands.)*

KEVIN. Yes? What is it?

MONTCRIEF. Have you seen an elderly woman around here?

KEVIN. *(sighs)* No.

MONTCRIEF. *(disappointed)* Oh.

KEVIN. *(helpfully)* It's a Nursing Home, I'm sure you could find another one.

MONTCRIEF. I'm looking for Mrs. Muir. She's one of our night owls. *(She turns the lights back on.)* Do you mind if we leave these on? If she sees them out, she comes in an talks to her imaginary friends.

KEVIN. Have you heard anything about my mother?

MONTCRIEF. No word. I'll check back.

KEVIN. Thank you. *(She leaves.)* How long am I going to have to sit here? *(He blinks up at the lights.)* ...working on my tan...

(He crosses to the lights, turns them off. He sits, stretches his arm

over his head. He does not see JULIA as she enters. She is in her late 70's, with a great deal of animation . She places a pillow in the opposite chair, crosses to the window, than begins speaking toward the pillow.)

JULIA. *(with great relish and secrecy)* Nice day today, wasn't it? *(KEVIN, taken by surprise, jumps in his seat.)* I like to come here to the Solarium just before sunrise and see what kind of a day it's going to be. And if it's going to be a beautiful day, I can say, "Oh, it's going to be a beautiful day." It cheers me right up. You can't imagine. And if it's not...well, there's a game room. Are you from Michigan originally? *(KEVIN looks around to see if she is addressing anyone.)* I'm from the San Joaquin Valley. That's in California, where the weather's always beautiful. Ooh, but I like your weather here—one day sunny, next day snow, it's so...suspenseful, don't you think? *(SHE moves closer to him. HE freezes.)* And there are worse places to live, you know. Take Alaska, for instance. Do you know people actually *live* up there? They do. *(Abruptly, SHE crosses to the magazine rack, HE evades her, still unnoticed.)* Thousands of them. I heard of people going up there, but I thought it was just a fad, you know? *(SHE leafs through a National Geographic. KEVIN watches her.)* Wow. Look at that. Mrs. Mueller, who lived on this floor until she died? She has a son who owns a shop up there. And he's not the only one. *National Geographic* says Alaska is one of our fastest-growing states.

KEVIN. *(fascinated)* Huh. *(He realizes what he has done and moves to the other side of the room.)*

JULIA. *(to the pillow)* That's right. *(Looks back at the*

magazine, then at the pillow, suspiciously. SHE shrugs and resumes.) I don't mean to complain, of course, but wouldn't it be an adventure to live somewhere else? Like Alaska? *(Crosses to the window.)* Far away from here, with the wind and the snow, and the caribou? Walking across the frozen bundra?

KEVIN. Tundra.

JULIA. Tundra? *(Pause. SHE turns to him and shrieks.)*

KEVIN. You must be Mrs. Muir. I didn't mean to frighten you.

JULIA. You frightened me.

KEVIN. I'm sorry. *(pause)* My name is Kevin.

JULIA. Oh. Hello.

KEVIN. Hello. *(pause)*

JULIA. You're not a killer, are you Kevin?

KEVIN. No.

JULIA. *(pause)* We had a killer on this floor last year.

KEVIN. You did? *(SHE nods.)*

JULIA. His name was Bob, though.

KEVIN. Well, I'm not here to kill anybody. My mother had a stroke.

JULIA. *(relieved)* Oh, that's good. I mean—

KEVIN. *(sympathetically)* I know what you mean. It's okay. I didn't mean to interrupt— *(starts to leave)*

JULIA. Where are you going?

KEVIN. I can find someplace else to wait.

JULIA. NO! *(catching herself)* I mean...no. You can stay if you want to.

KEVIN. *(delicately)* Don't you want to...you know...talk to your... *(Gestures with his head to the pillow.)* ...friend? *(She looks at the pillow.)*

JULIA. That's a pillow. I'd rather talk to you. Please stay.

KEVIN. Alright. *(HE sits. SHE stares at him.)*

JULIA. I've seen you before...

KEVIN. You have?

JULIA. Haven't I? Oh, well... *(excitedly)* You're here now. That's what's amazing.

KEVIN. Amazing?

JULIA. The fact that you're here. And I'm here. *(pause)*

KEVIN. We're both here.

JULIA. I knew you'd understand! Destiny brought us together—our paths were destined to cross, and a reason greater than ourselves has guided your path to me.

KEVIN. The cafeteria was closed. *(pause)*

JULIA. Or it could be something like that. *(HE chuckles. Urgently:)* You don't think I'm looney, do you?

KEVIN. No, I'm just not a believer in destiny.

JULIA. Well, I'm not looney.

KEVIN. I never said you were—

JULIA. That's 4-East. Senility patients. They used to think I belonged there, because I *(indicating the pillow)* like to talk. *(secretly)* But those poor people aren't with it.

KEVIN. No.

JULIA. I'm with it.

KEVIN. I see.

JULIA. I don't belong on 4-East. I'm not looney. I just come here to practice my conversation in case I get visitors like you.

KEVIN. How nice.

JULIA. Or the angels. *(pause)* Now you're looking at me

like I'm looney. *(KEVIN rises, crosses to the door to look outside.)*

KEVIN. Oh no, just thinking about my mother, is all.

JULIA. Do you believe in angels?

KEVIN. I haven't really thought about it.

JULIA. Think about it. *(Pause. SHE looks at him.)* What about it?

KEVIN. *(little laugh)* I don't know.

JULIA. Well, I believe in them. That's a secret. *(SHE takes him towards the window.)* Look out on the horizon. Isn't that beautiful?

KEVIN. It's very nice.

JULIA. Especially at dawn. Oh, you should see the dawn! I look at that, and at things around here— the beauty of springtime, the way a kind word feels. Hot tubs. And I have to think that it's all here for a reason.

KEVIN. I don't think everything is...meant to be—

JULIA. Like the way destiny threw us together? I think there is a reason in that.

KEVIN. The cafeteria was closed.

JULIA. But who closed it?

KEVIN. Janitors. *(pause)*

JULIA. I believe in them, too. *(HE laughs.)* What's wrong with your mother? *(HE stops laughing.)*

KEVIN. Well, she's—well, they're not sure. It may be a stroke.

JULIA. You must be very worried. *(HE starts to speak.)* Do you want to vent? *Current Psychology's* latest issue says you should vent your anxieties, and, if you want a good vent, you can trust me.

KEVIN. *(for lack of anything to say)* Well, the doctor's...looking at her now.

JULIA. *(gasping suddenly)* You're Margaret Birne's son!

KEVIN. Kevin Birne. Do you know my mother?

JULIA. I know both of you! *(Brings him back to the window.)* I watch from up here when you come to visit! I *knew* I recognized that scalp! *(She pulls his head forward, looks at the top of it.)* Oh, yes! Kevin Birne! Monday at four, right?

KEVIN. That's right!

JULIA. Oh, you have lovely ties.

KEVIN. Thank you.

JULIA. And your mother is having a stroke. *(pause)* That's not good.

KEVIN. No, but she's a tough lady. She'll see it through.

JULIA. *(sits him down)* Well, I can comfort you while you're waiting—

KEVIN. I'm really not that worried anymore—

JULIA. Oh, of course you are. Strokes can be fatal! *(pause)* Bad thing to say.

KEVIN. It's okay. They're not even sure it's a stroke. And I wouldn't be surprised if it was a lot of nonsense to get me back.

JULIA. From what?

KEVIN. *(reluctantly)* Oh, we had a ...difference of opinion a couple of weeks ago.

JULIA. Is that when she threw the magazine?

KEVIN. You saw that?

JULIA. *(innocently)* No.

KEVIN. She said, "Don't come back until you're sorry."

JULIA. Would she do that?

KEVIN. She loves to get the last word...it.. *(laughs)* It wasn't even a major thing...I'm not the kind of lawyer she wants me to be.

JULIA. What kind of lawyer are you?

KEVIN. A schoolteacher. *(proudly)* Mom will be alright. It's not like her to leave an argument unfinished. *(pause)* Why don't we talk about something else?

JULIA. *(seizing the opportunity)* Want to hear about Alaska? It's America's last frontier. *(Pause, as SHE shows him the magazine.)* They're not all bad, you know.

KEVIN. *(looking at the magazine)* What?

JULIA. Strokes. Some aren't too bad. Not everyone is Mr. Nesbit.

KEVIN. What happened to Mr. Nesbit? *(pause)*

JULIA. *(uncomfortably)* "Alaska is almost twice the size of Texas..." *(He rises, checks his watch, crosses to the window. Tentatively:)* I had a stroke. *(HE looks at her. Quickly:)* Not that I'm complaining, of course. But I came through fine. *(pause)* I remember this sharp pain in my head...and numbness...and laughing.

KEVIN. Laughing?

JULIA. "Laugh at death," they say. I don't know who "they" are. I tried laughing. It didn't work. The doctor thought I was hyperventilating and put a bag over my head.

KEVIN. What was it like?

JULIA. An ordinary bag.

KEVIN. No, the stroke.

JULIA. Oh...I remember fading in and out...there was pain, but I think the scariest thing was the lack of control... *(catching herself)* Not that I'm complaining, of course. I just wanted to tell you that I pulled through, and I'm sure your mother will. I'll ask the angels—

KEVIN. *(distractedly)* Thank you—

JULIA. If that's what you want. *(silence)*

KEVIN. What does that mean?

JULIA. You seemed angry at her.

KEVIN. Not *that* angry—

JULIA. Sometimes the relationship gets hard. I see that a lot.

KEVIN. You think I want her to die?

JULIA. *(after a pause)* I said the wrong thing—

KEVIN. Yes, you did—

JULIA. Please don't leave—

KEVIN. *(agitated)* Would I be here if I wanted her to die? Tonight, and every other night, and day? Would I worry and wait on her and feel like hell most of the time, if—what kind of person would want her to die? *(silence)*

JULIA. I don't know.

MONTCRIEF. *(off)* Mrs. Muir?

JULIA. Oh, God, that's Ms. Montcrief. She'll take me back to bed. *(JULIA rises.)*

KEVIN. Maybe that's best—

JULIA. NO!

MONTCRIEF. *(off)* Mrs. Muir? Please come out.

JULIA. *(to KEVIN)* Please let me stay! Do you know the last time I had company?! Do you know who was President?

MONTCRIEF. *(off)* Do I have to come in there?

KEVIN. I need to be alone, Mrs. Muir.

JULIA. I can help you! Really I can!

MONTCRIEF. *(off)* Okay.

(Sound of footsteps approaching. JULIA hides.)

JULIA. *(to KEVIN)* Trust me. *(SHE ducks down behind the sofa.)*

(Enter MONTCRIEF.)

MONTCRIEF. Mrs. Muir, I— *(Sees KEVIN.)* Oh.

KEVIN. How is my mother?

MONTCRIEF. They've moved her for observation.

KEVIN. It's serious, then?

MONTCRIEF. Well, I don't know. It's standard procedure.

KEVIN. *(a bit testy)* I'd like you to check.

MONTCRIEF. I will. I'm still looking for Mrs. Muir. Have you seen her? *(pause)*

JULIA. *(Whispering, to KEVIN.)* She's gone to bed.

KEVIN. She's gone to bed.

MONTCRIEF. She has?

KEVIN. *(improvising)* There was someone—a woman in here, and...she went to bed.

MONTCRIEF. I'd better check her room, then. *(starts to leave)*

JULIA. *(whisper)* No!

KEVIN. NO! *(MONTCRIEF stops. Covering:)* She...said she was going to bed. She said..."I'm going to bed."

MONTCRIEF. Are you sure it was Mrs. Muir?

KEVIN. Positive. She introduced herself. She said,

"Hello, I'm Mrs. Muir ... and I'm going to bed."

MONTCRIEF. *(after a moment)* Good.

JULIA. *(whisper)* Good.

MONTCRIEF. One less thing I have to take care of.

KEVIN. Would you check on my mother for me now?

MONTCRIEF. Certainly. *(She starts to leave.)*

KEVIN. And Ms. Montcrief? *(SHE stops.)* I want my mother to live. *(pause)*

MONTCRIEF. I'll let them know. *(SHE exits, JULIA comes out of hiding.)*

JULIA. Thank you. You're very kind.

KEVIN. No, I'm not. I'm sorry I raised my voice to you. And I'm sorry you think I hate my mother.

JULIA. I never said—

KEVIN. I don't, you know? It's just...sometimes she gets to me...I get angry...but I don't want her to die. She says things...*we* say things, that...she would never do anything to really hurt me. You know? I lose track of that sometimes, but that's my fault...I *do* love her...

JULIA. Have you told her that?

KEVIN. She knows.

JULIA. How?

KEVIN. A thousand different ways. I see her every Monday...I'm always there for her—a phone call—*(Snaps his fingers.)* and I'm here. Who else would do that for her?

JULIA. No one. *(pause)*

KEVIN. I may not be the best son in the world. *(laugh)* I may not even be a *good* one... *(Pause, quietly:)* But I do love her.

JULIA. Maybe you should tell her that.

KEVIN. She'll laugh in my face...

JULIA. Maybe. But she'll know. And you'll know you tried.

KEVIN. *(laughs)* You've got me hoping for something that'll never work...

JULIA. *(suddenly)* Did you know that Ancient Man thought every nightfall was his own death? *(Pause. He looks at her.)*

KEVIN. I was just now thinking of that.

JULIA. So was I! I read that, and I imagined how happy he must've been when he saw that little ribbon of dawn on the horizon. Another chance. Anything is possible with another chance.

KEVIN. *(smiling)* Even angels?

JULIA. Even angels.

(They laugh a moment, MONTCRIEF comes in, KEVIN moves between her and JULIA, as if to explain.)

MONTCRIEF. Mr. Birne? Dr. Costas will see you now.

KEVIN. *(smiles at JULIA)* Gotta go. Thank you. *(Heads for the door, to MONTCRIEF)* Is he in my mother's room?

MONTCRIEF. He's downstairs.

KEVIN. Well, can I see my mother first? *(Pause, to both of them.)* Whatever happened, I'm sure her version is a lot better than his. *(Pause. To MONTCRIEF.)* Hello?

MONTCRIEF. *(taking his arm gently)* I think we'd better go downstairs.

KEVIN. I'd like to see her first. Wait. *(HE removes his arm gently.)* What has happened?

MONTCRIEF. *(gently)* Your mother had a cerebral hemorrhage. We called an ambulance to take her to City Hospital—

KEVIN. Is she there?

MONTCRIEF. She died while we were moving her. *(silence)*

KEVIN. *(softly)* She *died?*

MONTCRIEF. I'm very sorry. It was apparently very quick, she—

KEVIN. *(to himself)* Just like that... *(crosses to the window)*

MONTCRIEF. Dr. Costas is waiting downstairs. He wants to talk to you. *(pause)* If you could come with me...

KEVIN. I...need some time. I'll see him in a minute... Please. *(beat)*

MONTCRIEF. Alright. We'll be downstairs. *(She exits. Long pause.)*

JULIA. I'm sorry.

KEVIN. *(stunned)* I should have seen it coming.

JULIA. I'm sorry about her. I'm not sorry for her. She's in a better place. You should know that...but you're angry. You must be. If you need to vent—

KEVIN. Leave me alone. Okay? Take your magazines and your stories and go back to bed.

JULIA. Don't send me back! Not when I can help! You need me!

KEVIN. *(controlling himself)* You can't help me. Go away—

JULIA. This doesn't mean you didn't love her—!

KEVIN. *(angry)* What does that matter now? Tell me! Come up with some story or magazine article on it! *(HE turns away from her. Quietly:)* You don't make people hope against the facts, lady. And the fact is she died because it was the last way she could really *get* me—

JULIA. People don't die for spite, Kevin—

KEVIN. Just LEAVE, OKAY? You couldn't understand! *(angrily)* Maybe I didn't give her too much to live for, but I didn't give her cause to die! *(silence)*

JULIA. "I'm very proud of my boy." *(pause)*

KEVIN. *(distantly)* What?

JULIA. "I'm very proud of my boy." She said it.

KEVIN. Who?

JULIA. Your mother. *(HE looks at her.)*

KEVIN. You didn't know her.

JULIA. I heard her. In the cafeteria. Everybody did. I didn't know her well, but someone like that wouldn't die for spite. *(pause)*

KEVIN. You're lying.

JULIA. I swear. *(pause)*

KEVIN. *(with difficulty)* She never said that to me.

JULIA. Maybe she never could. *(pause)* "I'm very proud of my boy."

KEVIN. *(smiling)* I'm proud of her, too. *(HE cries a little. SHE holds his hand. Little laugh.)* Maybe you're right about destiny. *(SHE smiles.)* Still don't believe in angels, though.

JULIA. *(softly)* Oh, you would be surprised where you can find angels these days.

BLACKOUT

SCENE TWO

A large,semi-private room in the Nursing Home. Enter SUTTON, a tall, pregnant nurse pushing JACK in a wheelchair. JACK is 82 and in a bad mood.

SUTTON. How was therapy today, Mr. C?

JACK. A joy.

SUTTON. I'm so glad. *(SHE escorts him, without touching him, to the bed.)*

JACK. It's so comforting to know that, at eighty-two, I'm still limber enough to have my left arm wrapped around my right shoulder by that sweaty dago with a third-grade education. *(SUTTON has started cranking the bed. JACK reaches for the handle.)* Give me that.

SUTTON. *(as JACK cranks)* Dr. Geraldo is a licensed physical therapist and you don't like him because he does what's good for you.

JACK. I don't like him because he smells like old food. Three times a week I'm left feeling like I've been wrestling with a giant summer sausage. Give me that. *(HE finishes cranking and gets into bed. SUTTON reads his chart.)*

SUTTON. That's not high enough.

JACK. It *is* high enough. I know what I like.

SUTTON. Not if you want to watch TV.

JACK. Who says I want to watch TV? TV is shit!

SUTTON. Okay, but I'm not going to answer your bell this afternoon when *Jeopardy's* on and you can't see it. *(pause)*

JACK. *(getting back out)* Bitch. Ball-busting bitch. *(SHE goes to crank the bed. He ushers her away, and does it himself.)*

SUTTON. *(sweetly)* I'm only doing this for you.

JACK. *(mimicking her)* "I'm only doing this for you." You people... *(as HE cranks)* I get screwed in this dump eighty ways to Sunday and all the time you so modestly say that it's all for my own good. *(HE stops cranking, looks at her.)* Vito Corleone pounds his olive-oil mitts into my miserable weak back until I bleed—but it's all for my own good. *(He tests the height—not high enough.)* That crazed Iranian—who is either a fag or a rapist, I can't tell—comes around once a month to make sure the bed pans are kept real cold and real full. *(HE stops. Stands.)* For my own good. *(HE stands, keeping SUTTON away and straightening his own sheets.)* And Hartmann! The Nazi proctologist with the cold hands and the huge suppositories, never misses a visit—because the world would stop turning if I had less than a pound of wax up my ass each week. I thank you all... *(HE gets back into bed, sitting up.)* And when you're burning in hell, Sutton, I will be the one poking your raisin-sized tits with a pitchfork, screaming: "Remember me?" *(to the bed)* There.

SUTTON. Someday you'll thank me for the way I baby you.

JACK. Someday I'll understand why your balls are bigger than mine, but neither day will come soon. *(As SHE bends over a tray.)* Say, how often are you banging your husband, now that you're six months in the oven? *(HE slaps her behind.)*

SUTTON. *(recoiling)* You're a lousy old prick, is what you are!

JACK. *(delighted)* What?

SUTTON. Prick! *(JACK laughs.)* Sometimes I think you're positively demonic.

JACK. What a terrible word.

SUTTON. "Demonic?"

JACK. "Sometimes." *(laughs)*

SUTTON. *(Putting his chart back.)* Well, I think that does it for now. Mrs. Muir will be back from dialysis soon, so you'll have her to abuse for awhile.

JACK. She was due up at 3:30. It's 3:37.

SUTTON. I'll send someone down for her. She's expecting a friend, she said. *(HE snorts.)* You'll have company.

JACK. *She'll* have company. I want no part of that crap.

SUTTON. Well, that's his loss, I'm sure. *(As SHE departs, with his tray.)* I don't know how anyone can go without the pleasure of your company.

JACK. Fuck off.

SUTTON. *(Laughing as she exits.)* I love you, too. *(JACK reaches over to his bedside table for something. It is not there. He curses to himself, thrusts open the drawer and feels around blindly. HE pulls out what he thinks is the TV remote control, points it towards the television and presses it. Unfortunately it is a Kleenex box. He looks at it.)*

JACK. FUCK! *(throws it away)* Julia, you bitch! Where did you put my remote control? *(HE shifts uncomfortably in the bed, reaches down under his legs and pulls out the remote control. He looks at it.)* Oh. *(He sniffs it, shrugs, presses, and we hear the TV come on. He sighs, leans back, pulls out a pack of hidden cigarettes and lights one.)* At last.

(Knock at the door.)

JACK. FUCK! *(HE hastily extinguishes the cigarette.)*

(KEVIN enters carrying some flowers and a box of candy, tied with a ribbon. JACK turns off the TV hastily and regards him, ominously.) What?

KEVIN. Excuse me, I was wondering—

JACK. WHAT?!

KEVIN. I was looking for Mrs. Muir. Julia Muir.

JACK. She's dead.

KEVIN. *(shocked)* WHAT?!

JACK. She's dead. I killed her. Cut her up. Put her in a shoe box. Sorry.

KEVIN. Who are you?

JACK. Mr. Muir. What the hell are you doing seeing my wife behind my back?

KEVIN. She's not dead.

JACK. No, but she won't last long in that shoe box, so you better talk fast.

KEVIN. *(with difficulty)* I'm a friend of hers.

JACK. No you're not.

KEVIN. *(hesitantly)* Yes, I am.

JACK. Are you contradicting me?

KEVIN. *(flustered)* No.

JACK. Yes you are!

KEVIN. No I'm not!

JACK. *(loudly)* Now! Now you're contradicting me! How dare you?

KEVIN. Maybe I have the wrong room...

JACK. Oh, you have the right room if you're here to

fuck my wife on the sly—

KEVIN. I never—!

JACK. *(miserably)* Oh, I knew it would be someone like you. She always had a weakness for skinny teen-age hard-ons with bad eating habits—

KEVIN. I'm—I never...I'm just visiting her. She might not have known I was coming—

JACK. Ooooh, here to seduce her, are you? In front of her husband's eyes, you *prick!* Where do you get the nerve? Perhaps an old man with a weak heart and Mafia ties doesn't frighten you—

KEVIN. Calm down!

JACK. —but I'm still a man, damn you! Heart condition or no, and I'll be *damned* if I will stand by—!!! *(HE breaks off suddenly, clutching his heart.)*

KEVIN. What? What is it? What's the matter? *(JACK holds his chest, eyes afire, mouthing words frantically.)*

JACK. *(hoarsely)* Mother! Mother! I hear you, Mother!

KEVIN. Oh *GOD!*

JACK. *(serenely slumping into bed)* I see a faint glow above my head...a tunnel...

KEVIN. *(frantic)* What should I do? I'll get a nurse— *(starts to leave)*

JACK. NO!! *(HE stops.)* You'll be too late.

KEVIN. OH *GOD!!! (KEVIN helps JACK position himself on the bed.)*

JACK. *(faintly)* Sugar! My blood is thin.

KEVIN. *(to himself)* Sugar! Where can I get some?

JACK. Candy is good.

KEVIN. Candy is good! *(HE grabs his candy box. The wrapper won't give.)* Can't get the wrapper—

JACK. Mama!

KEVIN. *(frantically)* FUCK THE WRAPPER! *(He smashes the candy box open on the side of the bed. Candy flies everywhere. He grabs some and thrusts them toward JACK'S mouth.)*

JACK. *(Faintly, through candy)* I prefer the creams.

KEVIN. Just eat.

JACK. And crank up the bed.

KEVIN. Crank it up. Right.

(He does so as SUTTON enters.)

KEVIN. Nurse, thank God you're here. This man is having a heart attack—! *(SUTTON, oblivious to him, crosses directly to JACK and interrupts KEVIN.)*

SUTTON. *(taking candy from him)* Mr. Corrigan, I told you you can't have candy. It's not in your diet! *(SHE leaves. JACK sits up, suddenly very alive.)*

JACK. *(as she leaves)* BITCH!! *(Oblivious of KEVIN, he picks up the remote control, turns on the TV and begins to watch. Pause.)*

KEVIN. *(For lack of anything to say.)* Well, thank you. Thank you for making a fool out of me.

JACK. Don't be modest, kid, you made a fool out of yourself. I just watched. *(He watches TV.)*

KEVIN. I was told Mrs. Julia Muirs' room was 412. Now, is it or isn't it? *(JACK watches TV. KEVEN marches to the TV, shuts if off.)* Is this Mrs. Muir's room? *(JACK turns the set back on with the remote control. KEVIN switches it off. JACK switches it on. KEVIN switches it off. JACK switches it on, KEVIN turns if off and turns the set to face the wall.)*

JACK. Prick.

KEVIN. I'm at the end of my patience with you, Mister! You wreck my candy, you make me—AAAGH! All I want is a civil answer to a civil question—Now—WHERE DO I FIND MRS. MUIR?! *(pause)*

JACK. *(feeble)* I'm...sorry, young man. I didn't mean to irritate you...I just lost control of myself. *(pause)*

KEVIN. Well...that's alright...

JACK. You're the first real visitor I've had in eight years. My son used to visit me when he was on leave, but he died in Viet Nam, you see. My daughter-in-law pays the bills, but when it comes to visits, she and I never really...

KEVIN. *(reluctantly)* I'm sorry.

JACK. No, *I'm* sorry. I shouldn't— *(He coughs. A horrible cough.)* I shouldn't be so.eccentric. *(hoarsely)* Could you come a little closer, please? I'm not supposed to raise my voice. *(KEVIN does.)* Mrs. Muir is a lovely lady, don't you think?

KEVIN. Yes.

JACK. A lovely lady, to be sure. *(indulgent and feeble)* And you want to see her?

KEVIN. Yes. *(JACK nods, reaches under the bed, and with malicious joy produces a shoe-box. He opens one end, peers inside.)*

JACK. *(calling)* Mrs. Muir! *(to KEVIN)* Which parts do you want to see? *(He laughs at KEVIN, who steps away.)*

KEVIN. Isn't it about time for your nap or something?

JACK. Fuck you.

(Enter JULIA, SUTTON guiding her.)

JULIA. Kevin! How wonderful of you to come! *(SHE crosses to him feebly and embraces him.)* You've met Mr. Corrigan, then? *(SHE goes to sit.)*

JACK. Such a nice young man.

KEVIN. *(to JACK)* Drop dead.

JULIA. Oh, good. I see you've had a chance to talk.

SUTTON. Mr. Corrigan had a cardiac arrest today.

JULIA. Oh really? *(to KEVIN)* Kevin, I'm sorry. I should have been here.

SUTTON. You usually hemmorrhage for first-time visitors.

JACK. I know. Today I felt a little tired. Four-eyes really went for it, though. *(KEVIN makes to speak. JULIA finds several candies underfoot.)*

JULIA. Oh, Kevin, were these for me?

KEVIN. They were.

JULIA. Oh, thank you dear. I love creams.

KEVIN. They were a mixed assortment.

JULIA. Oh. Well. *(pointing)* Somebody stepped on a cream here. *(SUTTON begins picking them up.)*

KEVIN. I'm sorry you can't eat them now—

JACK. Sutton can though, can't she? Why bother to pick them up with your fingers, Sutton? Why not just kneel down and graze?

SUTTON. *(laughing)* For your information, Mr. Corrigan, I'm going to throw these away.

JACK. The hell you are. You're going to sit on top of dispatch with that other miserable knocked-up nurse and cram them into your fat faces.

SUTTON. *(standing)* While we eat thick, greasy hamburgers, covered with tobasco sauce, *(JACK groans.)* and talk of Jack Corrigan, our favorite patient in the whole wide world. *(SHE tosses him one piece of candy, heads out.)*

JACK. *(calling)* I hope the baby is born with horns!

SUTTON. Only if the father is you. *(exits)*

JULIA. *(laughing)* I think Karen has your number, Jack.

JACK. Fuck her. No one has my number. Not even you.

JULIA. *(to KEVIN)* This is such an exciting day for me. And the best part of it all is having a visitor. *(SHE takes his arm.)* How are you?

KEVIN. I'm fine. And you look well.

JULIA. Oh, pshaw, I'm a mess with what I've been through today.

KEVIN. What have you been—?

JULIA. —thank you just the same. How about your mother? Did the funeral go off alright? *(to JACK)* We met in the Solarium the night Kevin's mother passed away—

JACK. I know.

KEVIN. Everything went fine. Really. You said you went through something today. Are you alright?

JULIA. *(crossing toward the table)* Oh, poof. Dialysis three times a week. No big deal.

KEVIN. Dialysis. I'm sorry. I forgot what that means.

JULIA. *(gently)* It means I can't eat candy.

KEVIN. I'm sorry.

JACK. She can't eat candy, and she's too old to get laid.

JULIA. Jack—

JACK. You're barking up the wrong tree, kid.

JULIA. Jack, Are you jealous because I have a visitor?

JACK. *(offended)* Certainly not.

JULIA. Jack, I want to—

JACK. If you think I'd be jealous of that—

JULIA. Jack, I want to have a *nice* conversation with my friend here. If you'd like to join us, you are surely welcome. *(Pause. JACK rises, gets on his robe with difficulty.)* Where are you going?

JACK. I'm going to wrestle Sutton for candy. I hope you have fun, but don't blame me when he puts his hand on your ass. *(HE goes.)*

JULIA. *(calling after him:)* You're supposed to take a wheelchair.

KEVIN. Did I offend him?

JULIA. I think not.

KEVIN. Too bad.

JULIA. He gets feisty, I know, but he's really a good man.

KEVIN. I can't believe he's your husband.

JULIA. *(laughs)* Jack? Oh, Good Lord, did he tell you that?

KEVIN. He told me a lot things.

JULIA. Well! I have something to tell you. Guess what?

KEVIN. What?

JULIA. *(with great satisfaction)* I knew you were coming today. That's right. I was watching the sun come up today—it was especially beautiful today, the way the sky turned a pale violet, and the clouds just seemed to catch fire—and I heard myself say, "Today will be special," and my eyes fell on your chair in the Solarium. Something about you was still there, Kevin—an aura is what they call it in books. And your aura told me you would be here. And here you are! *(pause)*

KEVIN. I called you yesterday.

JULIA. *(confused)* You did? *(SHE tries to remember.)* Even better!

KEVIN. So what does that mean? You got my aura off the phone?

JULIA. I didn't even remember it! Isn't that wonderful?

KEVIN. So you got my aura off a chair? *(laughs)* Maybe they should use slipcovers. *(Pause. No response.)* Slipcovers...

JULIA. Oh, no. Those chairs are clean.

KEVIN. It was a joke.

JULIA. Oh. Ha ha ha ha ha! *(pause)*

KEVIN. Mrs. Muir—

JULIA. Julia—

KEVIN. Julia. I have some things to say.

JULIA. Great! *(Pause. He paces a bit.)*

KEVIN. First, I want to thank you for what you told me about my mother. I would never have known otherwise...

JULIA. She was very proud of you—

KEVIN. —And second, I want to apologize for being a rotten person the other night—

JULIA. I wouldn't say "rotten"—

KEVIN. I was rotten. No excuses. I said some things...about my mother, that, especially now seem... That was *not* me, okay? Believe me, you saw me at my worst. *(Pause. HE struggles for words.)*

JULIA. So are we friends now...or what?

KEVIN. Excuse me?

JULIA. Friends. I want us to be friends. *(HE starts to speak.)* I *know*—I saw you at your worst. *(simply—)* I want us to be friends. *(pause)*

KEVIN. *(carefully)* Alright. *(laugh)* Sure.

JULIA. *(with great excitement)* Great! We're friends! And you'll come see me, and we'll have long conversations, and you'll loan me huge amounts of money!

KEVIN. *(uncomfortable)* Excuse me?

JULIA. *(quoting:)* "A friend is a blessing of quiet solace, and a tranquil coupling of souls..."

KEVIN. That's pretty. Who said that?

JULIA. Jack did.

KEVIN. *(dully)* Oh. *(pause)* So. I've already come to see you. What part are we on now?

JULIA. Um—long conversations.

KEVIN. Long conversations. Right. *(Pause. Both stare at each other.)* Aren't—aren't you going to start?

JULIA. Should I?

KEVIN. Don't you always?

JULIA. No, just with pillows. You have to start with pillows, or you never get anything going. *(pause)* I think we're both nervous.

KEVIN. I'm sure there are thousands of things to talk about.

JULIA. *(after a pause)* So.

KEVIN. So... *(Pause. HE stands, paces the room more.)* Nice room.

JULIA. Thank you...it's the Nursing Home's.

KEVIN. Well, yes, but I can see little touches of you here and there.

JULIA. Oh, thank you! *(pause)* Where?

KEVIN. *(Hastily looking around the room.)* Well, this picture, for instance, is very lovely. Is it yours?

JULIA. *(tactfully)* Yes and no. The angle its hung at is mine. *(looking at it)* It must be a very expensive picture, the way its wired into the wall. One of these days, when I have enough strength, I'm going to twist those wires so they hang straight.

KEVIN. *(sympathetically)* How *are* you feeling?

JULIA. Oh, fine. *(pause)*

KEVIN. That's it?

JULIA. *(puzzled)* How should I feel?

KEVIN. No, you usually ask...elderly people how they feel and you get a long sermon. *(Pause. HE laughs. Pause.)*

JULIA. Oh. Not me. I'm fine. *(HE is disappointed.)* There are certain times when I'm feeling really bad, of course. But they always pass.

KEVIN. Certain times? *(SHE nods.)* And what are they like? *(pause)*

JULIA. Really bad.

KEVIN. *(sigh)* I see. *(HE rises again, pacing uncomfortably)*

JULIA. Kevin, what is wrong?

KEVIN. I don't know. It's not you. It's me. Again. Really.

JULIA. I'm having fun.

KEVIN. No, you're not! I mean...maybe you are, but...

JULIA. But what?

KEVIN. I'm sorry. I don't feel comfortable, Julia. I

never felt comfortable here. I'm sorry, Julia, I promised I'd make this a nice visit. I owe you that, don't I? I had this whole thing planned out on the way over...you should have been there, you had a great time.

JULIA. I'm glad.

KEVIN. I...wish I could just relax here, you know? I can't seem to do anything right these days. *(Pause. Suddenly, JULIA starts laughing.)*

JULIA. Slipcovers. I just got that.

KEVIN. Julia, have you been listening to me?

JULIA. No. I've been watching you. I like to do that. I watch people when they come to the nurse's station. Can't hear what they say...but I can see what they feel. Confusion, or anger—they're easy to tell—so are people who really don't care. I pick *them* out even better than Jack. But I wouldn't pick you.

KEVIN. I'm just not—

JULIA. Kevin. If you came to "pay me what you owe me," stick to your plan. Talk nice to me, ask me how I'm feeling, and leave. *(shrugs)* People do it all the time. *(carefully)* If you want to be my friend, just stay with me awhile. Good mood, bad mood, I don't care. Just...be with me. *(pause)*

KEVIN. We have nothing in common, you know.

JULIA. I know. I'm a woman, you're a man—

KEVIN. Yes—

JULIA. I'm old and you're young—

KEVIN. *(reluctantly)* Yes. *(pause)*

JULIA. *(innocently)* I've slept with Perry Como, and I'll bet you haven't.

KEVIN. Is that true?

JULIA. *(laughing)* No. But I made it up one Christmas to shock people, and, you know, it works.

KEVIN. That's terrible. *(THEY both laugh.)*

JULIA. I know. I told it to Jack once and he fell out of bed. *(KEVIN laughs. Solemnly.)* If he hadn't've broken his toe, it would have been really funny. *(Pause. BOTH laugh.)* Stop it now. *(still laughing)* It was really serious.

KEVIN. *(laughter subsiding)* Hey, *I'm* supposed to cheer *you* up.

JULIA. Cheering up people is what I do best.

KEVIN. I envy you. I'm not very good with people. But then I don't really have to be...

JULIA. What do you do?

KEVIN. I'm a schoolteacher. *(Pause. THEY both laugh.)* That sounds terrible, doesn't it? I teach English, you see, and it doesn't really matter what *I'm* like. It's Walt Whitman, or William Faulkner, or whoever we're learning ...see, *they* care if they know *you* care, and—

JULIA. I'll bet you're a good teacher.

KEVIN. *(off-guard)* Well, I—I don't know. I never think of it in those terms, but...yes, *(Uncomfortably, laughing.)* God, I come to visit and wind up talking about me. What about you? What...do you...?

JULIA. I told you. I cheer people up.

KEVIN. *(laughs)* Is that it?

JULIA. Isn't that enough? *(HE laughs, SHE seems a bit uncomfortable.)* I did other things of course, but...I'm too old for them now...

KEVIN. Older people work past retirement these days. Maybe you could go back to work.

JULIA. I don't think that's possible... *(She eyes the dancer figurine on the table.)*

KEVIN. Why not?

JULIA. *(an idea)* I was a dancer. *(HE laughs.)* Really, I was. After I got out of high school and before I got married. It was hard work... *(savoring this:)* But the way a dancer moves onstage, spinning and flying and reaching out...like magic they weave through space...I only actually danced for a little while. Then I became a telephone operator, then a grocery store clerk, and then a wife...but I always like to think of myself as a dancer. *(pause)*

KEVIN. Maybe you could leave here. *(Surprised, SHE looks at him, laughs.)* Get some kind of outpatient status and live on your own.

JULIA. And do what?

KEVIN. Don't you have ambitions?

JULIA. Yes, I do. I want to be a dancer.

KEVIN. Okay, maybe that's not possible—

JULIA. *(interrupting)* In your world, no. But in mine...I still dance. In my own way.

(As JACK enters, unnoticed.)

KEVIN. I can't help thinking you'd be happier out there, in a world full of people...people who would love you. *(HE checks his watch.)*

JULIA. You really think so?

KEVIN. We'll talk about it on our next visit. Right now, I've got to go. *(HE stands.)*

JULIA. *(standing)* When will you be back?

KEVIN. *(casually)* Soon.

JULIA. But you can't name a day?

KEVIN. *(laughing)* Soon, I promise. Will you walk me out?

JACK. Sutton wants you in the Solarium first. You left your purse there.

JULIA. *(to KEVIN)* Oh, dear. That's the other way. *(to JACK)* Now?

JACK. She's locking up. It's your fucking handbag.

JULIA. *(to KEVIN)* Do you mind if we say goodbye here? *(HE shakes his head.)* And I'll see you soon?

KEVIN. Alright.

JULIA. Good. *(She hugs him quickly and leaves.)*

KEVIN. Goodbye, Jack.

JACK. Stay.

KEVIN. Another cardiac arrest? *(JACK retrieves the purse, which has been hidden under his robe, and tosses it on JULIA'S bed.)*

JACK. What do you want, hard-on?

KEVIN. Nothing. Not from you.

JACK. What do you want from her?

KEVIN. I don't want anything from her—

JACK. Bullshit. *(pause)* Maybe you're thinking: "Old woman, sick woman, no relatives in sight—" She has no money to speak of, I can tell you that—

KEVIN. *(indignant)* I wouldn't touch her money—

JACK. No, I didn't think you would. You're too whitebread for that, aren't you? You're worse. You're thinking you can save her. Or save yourself.

KEVIN. I don't know what you're talking about—

JACK. People like you have something to prove, something on their conscience. Maybe they want to think of themselves as philanthropic. Or maybe they just want to be mothered—

KEVIN. You leave my mother out of this!

JACK. I don't give a good crap about your mother and I don't give a good crap about you! But people like you use people like her to prove something to yourselves, and the moment you do you waltz off into the sunset, leaving the likes of her in places like this wondering what the hell they did wrong. Now I don't give a good fuck if I see your lousy face again or not... *(Pause. HE touches her bed.)* But she's different. She still thinks people are kind. What I mean is, if you say you're going to show up, you damn well better show up. *(pause)*

KEVIN. You'd like it if I didn't.

JACK. Try me, asshole.

(KEVIN leaves. JACK gets in bed. After a moment, JULIA re-enters.)

JULIA. Karen says she gave it to you. *(JACK points to the purse on the bed. JULIA looks at it confused.)* Oh. Is he gone? *(no answer)* I think he's very sweet.

JACK. He told me he gets hot thinking of your saggy white thighs.

JULIA. Jack, now stop that. You'll get to like him. I know. *(JACK picks up the remote control and turns on the TV.)*

JACK. Not a chance.

(LIGHTS fade on everything but the glow of the television as JULIA goes into the bathroom to change.)

SCENE THREE

A couple weeks later. JACK is in bed. JULIA changing in the bathroom. Enter MONTCRIEF.

MONTCRIEF. Good morning, Mr. Corrigan. I want to talk to Mrs. Muir before I punch out. *(She looks at JULIA'S empty bed.)* She's off again, isn't she?

JACK. She's in the bathroom. *(MONTCRIEF checks her watch.)*

MONTCRIEF. Now? Isn't that unusual?

JACK. No. I've heard of other people going to the bathroom. It's a popular thing.

MONTCRIEF. I mean at this time of morning. *(To JULIA, through the bathroom door.)* I think all her late nights have put her off her schedule.

JULIA. *(off)* I'm just watering some flowers.

JACK. Oh, leave her be, Montcrief. Maybe she likes her late nights. *(pause)* You seem to like yours.

MONTCRIEF. What's that supposed to mean?

JACK. It means every night you're coming in with darker circles under your eyes, and every day that Orderly's smile gets a little bigger. I can put two and two together.

MONTCRIEF. *(evasive)* I have no idea what you're talking about.

JACK. He said you'd say that. He said some other things, too, like—

(JULIA enters from the bathroom with KEVIN'S flowers.)

JACK. —can't talk now. Mixed company. *(winks)*

MONTCRIEF. You're lying.

JACK. I am. And I'm very sorry.

(Enter ORDERLY, with tray. Very friendly:)

JACK. Hello!

ORDERLY. *(Confused, looks at both of them.)* Hello.

JACK. Let's see a big smile. *(ORDERLY smiles broadly. JACK smiles broadly. BOTH smile broadly at MONTCRIEF.)*

ORDERLY. *(innocently)* Anything to clean in here?

MONTCRIEF. *(To ORDERLY as SHE leaves.)* You shit! *(ORDERLY looks desperately to JACK.)*

ORDERLY. *(After she leaves, tentatively:)* ...I guess not... *(Exits. JULIA crosses to her table with a brush.)*

JACK. What are you getting all gussied up for?

JULIA. Nothing special.

JACK. *(mimicking)* Nothing special...I can tell when your boyfriend's coming. You put on that "little old lady" voice.

JULIA. Maybe I have a little old lady voice because I'm a little old lady.

JACK. Get out. What does that make me? A "little old man?" Maybe I should wear cardigan sweaters and listen to fucking Lawrence Welk while he's here.

JULIA. *(Starting to water the flowers again.)* Stop it, Jack.

JACK. I got news for you, anyway. It's only Monday. Thursday's your day to play den mother.

JULIA. He said he might come early this week.

JACK. And what if he doesn't show up today?

JULIA. Then he doesn't show up today. Today is just one day, is all.

JACK. *(Quoting MacBeth:)* "And tomorrow, and tomorrow..."

JULIA. *(going back to the bathroom)* You really don't like him, do you? Why?

JACK. He's human. I don't like anything about the mollusk class. Slugs you can trust.

JULIA. *(from the bathroom)* Why?

JACK. Because I don't like him, that's why! I don't like what he does to you...he changes you.

JULIA. *(Comes out of the bathroom. SHE looks pretty good.)* How do I look?

JACK. Like a prostitute.

JULIA. Thank you. *(Crosses to water the flowers.)*

JACK. You already watered those. *(SHE stops, confused.)*

JULIA. Oh. *(pause)* His flowers has lasted a week this time. I take that as a good omen.

JACK. Omens! What is all this shit suddenly with omens and signs? I never heard you say word one about that crap before the night his Mommy died, and now suddenly you're filled with enough hocus-pocus to be burned at Salem.

JULIA. It's not bad to have a religion.

JACK. Religion is legitimized hocus-pocus. Besides, you don't belong to any church.

JULIA. Why can't what I believe be its own religion?

JACK. Because you don't feel like hell! That's what religion is for, stupid! You're supposed to feel like hell.

And, if you don't, you're cheating millions of *really* religious people who work very hard everyday to feel like hell!

JULIA. Well, I'm not going to feel religious today. I've got too much to be happy about.

JACK. There you go with that "little old lady" schtick. I think I'll hire some Boy Scouts to help you across the street.

JULIA. *(angrily)* It bothers you so much that I'm happy!

JACK. It wouldn't bother me if I knew it was you! It wouldn't bother me if I knew it was the same woman who hated this place as much as I did, the same woman who I scream at nurses for, and taught to say "fuck" in physical therapy. Where did *she* go?

JULIA. Maybe this is a side of me you've never seen before.

JACK. Then how come I only see it on Thursdays? *(pause)* I don't believe this lame-brained, happy-go-lucky broad you cook up once a week. And he won't believe it forever.

JULIA. I don't know what you mean.

JACK. You talk about yourself like nothing scares you. Nothing hurts. Because you're terrified he'll find out it does and run from you like the plague.

JULIA. He doesn't need to hear that—

JACK. But you need to tell it. And instead you make yourself out like Tinkerbell in orthopedic hose. He'll see through that the same way he'll see through that mother crap you use.

JULIA. I knew Mrs. Birne—

JACK. You saw Margaret Birne maybe twice in the hallway. She was a snake in a four dollar house coat. She only opened her mouth to tell people off, or to swallow mice.

JULIA. That's not nice.

JACK. No, but it's honest. We know that. He will, too. It's just a matter of time.

JULIA. Jack, why do you do this? Don't ruin today for me, alright? I'm not the enemy—I don't deserve this from you.

JACK. How would you feel if he came in right now?

JULIA. Huh?

JACK. How would you feel if—?

JULIA. Pleased, I guess.

JACK. And how would you feel if I didn't ever warn you, and one day he stopped showing up?

JULIA. *(conceding)* Bad...

JACK. Bad?

JULIA. Real bad.

JACK. Maybe that's why I do that. *(HE grabs the remote control.)*

JULIA. And what should we do in the meantime?

JACK. *(Turning on the TV.)* "Television heals all wounds."

JULIA. *(Crossing to the TV.)* No, it doesn't. *(Switches it off. HE switches it back on. SHE switches it off, HE switches it back on. SHE switches it off. HE switches it back on, SHE switches it off, and sits on it. Blocking his view.)*

JACK. *(Angrily, tossing the remote control.)* Everybody does this to me!

JULIA. You didn't answer me.

JACK. Does one snotty-nosed teenager make you so tough?

JULIA. He's not a teenager and I'm not tough, now answer me. *(HE rises, starts crossing to her.)*

JACK. Answer you what, woman?

JULIA. What do we do in the meantime, if there's nothing to hope for? We spend most of our time in "the meantime," you know. I want to spend it hoping for something good. Why don't you?

JACK. Because it's farther to fall when nothing happens. Day after day after day.

JULIA. I'd rather take the risk.

JACK. Like with Lorraine? *(silence)*

JULIA. *(softly)* Lorraine was different.

JACK. How? *(no response)* How?

JULIA. *(Angrily)* She just was!

JACK. You mean she wasn't sincere? We both know she was, for the piss-poor lot sincerity will buy you. She was real sincere, with the bringing of the fruit baskets and the pictures of her kids, and the phone calls every Sunday night to see how we were. Remember when she showed us the shots of her farm? She said she'd take us out there one day—out in the fresh air, remember? And you bought right into it, and I bought right into it, too. And that was the last time she ever showed up. Sincerely.

JULIA. I don't think it was her fault.

JACK. Well it sure as shit wasn't ours!

JULIA. I know it's been a long time. Maybe she's just delayed.

JACK. Yeah. That's what they said about Amelia Earhart.

JULIA. Don't make jokes! You get me all upset and then you make jokes! Maybe it *was* our fault she left—I don't know! I only know I hate being lonely! *(cries)*

JACK. *(softer)* Come on, don't cry. *(pause)* That's a wood-grain Magnavox, you dumb broad, I don't want tears on it. *(SHE starts to get off.)* No, no. Don't get off if you don't want to. I didn't say get off. Stay there if you want. Probably the warmest place in the whole fucking room. *(Pause. HE looks at her.)* Julia? Are you horny? I could raise the antenna.

JULIA. *(laughing)* Are you trying to cheer me up?

JACK. Hell no! I don't care what you feel like! I just hate that god-awful snorting sound when you cry...sounds like bull-walruses in heat.

(SHE laughs, snorting involuntarily. HE snorts back at her. SUTTON enters to see them snorting at each other, and JULIA on the TV.)

SUTTON. What the hell is this?

JACK. What the hell does it look like? *(SUTTON looks at JULIA, who snorts.)* Julia has gastritis today.

SUTTON. So?

JACK. So, I'm trying to jump start my television set. *(JULIA, still laughing, starts to slide off the side of the TV. SUTTON catches her and stands her up. JACK gets back in bed.)* Women.

JULIA. Karen, will you help me to the bathroom? I have to freshen up.

SUTTON. Sure. *(She helps her to the bathroom.)*

JACK. I don't know if I'd let that big dyke in the same

john if I were you.

SUTTON. It's okay, pregnant dykes don't hurt anybody. *(With JULIA in the bathroom, she crosses to JACK, rolls up his sleeve and begins taking his blood pressure.)*

JACK. *(calling to JULIA:)* Hey, hurry up in there! A man's gotta pee, too, you know!

SUTTON. Mr. C, I wanted to warn you you'll have to simmer down for awhile. Nurse Raymond has taken a shift on this floor.

JACK. Who the hell is Nurse Raymond?

SUTTON. The nurse from 4 East you kicked last April.

JACK. Oh, her. That wasn't my fault. She used the editorial "we."

SUTTON. What do you mean?

JACK. You'd know if you had to listen to her for a week. "Mr. Corrigan, aren't WE happy?" "Don't WE want a tranquilizer?" "Shouldn't WE use a urinal?" I said, "You and I do not constitute "WE," then I kicked her in the shins and said, "See, *you* are in a lot of pain right now, but WE are enjoying the hell out of this."

SUTTON. Listen, I'm giving you fair warning. She's starting this afternoon and she's still pissed off at you. Now, that means rest, and if you so much as move from there, she'll be all over you like a rash. *(She gives him the urinal.)* And that means use your little friend, okay?

JACK. Where will you be?

SUTTON. I'm going home. My husband is sick.

JULIA. *(from the bathroom)* I hope it's nothing serious.

SUTTON. *(to JULIA)* No, it sounds like the flu.

JACK. He'll probably die.

JULIA. *(off)* JACK!

JACK. Will you get out of there? I have to piss!

SUTTON. Use the urinal.

JACK. Fuck you... *(begrudgingly)* and tell your fucking husband to get better and support his demon children like he's supposed to.

SUTTON. I will. Goodbye. *(She exits.)*

JULIA. *(off)* Goodbye, Karen.

JACK. Yeah. *(to JULIA:)* Will you get out of there?

JULIA. Right out.

JACK. *(mimicking her:)* "Right out"—you don't have a decent kidney, how long can it take? *(He fumbles for the remote control, can not find it.)* And where the hell is my remote control? I have to take a piss, I don't have any remote control... *(Quoting As You Like It:)* "Oh, how full of briars is this working-day world."

JULIA'S VOICE. Use the switches on the television.

JACK. Maybe I don't want to use the switches on the television. Maybe I don't want to move with watermelon kidneys!

JULIA'S VOICE. Right out.

JACK. Oh, fuck me. *(He rises, puts on his robe and heads out the door. Pause. Voice from the hallway:)*

JACK'S VOICE. *(tartly)* Hello, Raymond.

RAYMOND'S VOICE. What do you think you're doing?

JACK'S VOICE. Looking for a bathroom.

RAYMOND'S VOICE. Why?

JACK'S VOICE. Hold still and I'll show you. *(Voices get louder as they get closer.)*

RAYMOND'S VOICE. You're not supposed to be out here, Mr. Corrigan.

(They appear, RAYMOND holding JACK by the arm.)

RAYMOND. You're supposed to use a urinal.

JACK. I don't want to use a urinal! Let go of me, you bitch! I'm fully capable of using a bathroom! Don't you push me!

RAYMOND. We're going to play by hospital rules now, friend. We're not going to get away with the stunts we pulled last year.

JACK. Let go of me!

RAYMOND. Then follow orders and get into bed. *(HE does. SHE shows him the urinal.)* Do we know what to do with this?

JACK. We sure do. Bend over. *(She opens the robe, puts it under him.)* Ow! Shit!

RAYMOND. *(Pulling the covers and robe downstage to mask the following:)* Now go.

JACK. You can't—

RAYMOND. Yes, I can, Mr. Corrigan, and I'll stay right here until you do go. *(HE does.)* Good.

(JULIA coming out from the bathroom.)

JULIA. What's the commotion?

JACK. *(desperately)* Julia, stay in there!

RAYMOND. Come on out, Mrs. Muir, I'm just having Mr. Corrigan go to the bathroom.

JACK. *(over her line:)* Don't tell her! Julia, stay in there!

RAYMOND. Come on out, Mrs. Muir. *(Reluctantly, SHE does.)* Just concentrate on what you're doing Mr. Corrigan. *(to JULIA:)* Just someone using a urinal. I'm sure you've seen it a thousand times before.

JACK. *(humiliated)* You...bitch.

RAYMOND. *(surprised)* Now, you shouldn't be embarrassed. You two were the ones who wanted to share a "co-ed room," remember? You shouldn't be shy over a little bodily function. *(to JACK:)* I'm going to leave this here in case you go again, and if you *do* go again, use the urinal, *not* the bathroom, understood?

JACK. Understood.

RAYMOND. And if you need anything, use the buzzer. I don't want you out of that bed, clear? *(HE nods. SHE exits, leaving him staring at the dead TV.)*

JULIA. *(Gently, after a pause.)* Did you find your remote control? *(HE shakes his head, absently. Pause. His eyes take in the doorway and the sprinkler pipe above it, and mist over in thought. HE rises, with a detached grin.)* What are you thinking?

JACK. *(As he approaches the foot of the bed.)* "Beware thou, who chid'st me past the precipice of reason, with mine own nectar I shall foil thee..." *(to JULIA)* Know who said that?

JULIA. No.

JACK. *(unhooking the urinal)* I did. *(HE crosses to the door, hooking the urinal on the pipe so that the opened door will spill the contents.)*

JULIA. Jack—what are you—? Jack! Jack, no! *(HE heads back to the center of the room.)* You can't do this! You can't go through with this! *(HE gets into bed.)*

JACK. *(innocently)* Julia, have you seen my remote control? *(Mystified, SHE shakes her head.)* Neither have I. I'll have to ring for the Nurse. *(HE does.)*

JULIA. Jack, please! I can't be a party to this!

JACK. You weren't. You were asleep. *(SHE doesn't get it.)* Asleep! *(SHE rolls over, feigning sleep.)* Ha ha ha. Please, God, have your awful mouth open.

(Quite suddenly, KEVIN enters in a nice suit.)

KEVIN. *(coming through)* Hello! *(The urinal dumps on him, spilling everywhere. JULIA is quickly up.)*

JULIA. KEVIN!

JACK. *(deadpan)* Hi. *(KEVIN stands bewildered, JULIA comes to him with a towel, leads him over away from the mess.)*

JULIA. Oh, I'm so sorry, Kevin. Jack is sorry, too.

JACK. I am, kid. You weren't the primary target.

RAYMOND'S VOICE. *(off)* What's going on?

JACK. Speak of the devil.

KEVIN. Is this what I think it is, or am I just paranoid of hospital smells?

(RAYMOND appears at the doorway.)

RAYMOND. What's going on?

JACK. My bladder exploded. Thousands injured. Film at eleven.

RAYMOND. Alright, Mr. Corrigan, if we're going to make trouble— *(She slips on something near the bed and falls on the ground. RAYMOND and JULIA scream. The television clicks on.)*

KEVIN. *(to RAYMOND)* Are you alright?

RAYMOND. *(with fierce disgust)* I'm covered with piss!
JULIA. *(to JACK)* She found your remote control.
JACK. *(to the TV)* Sometimes there is a God.

END OF ACT ONE

ACT TWO
SCENE ONE

The Solarium, a few minutes later. Enter RAYMOND and JULIA. RAYMOND is walking somewhat uncomfortably.

RAYMOND. You can come in now. *(JULIA enters, still looking behind her.)* You'll have to wait here until the room is cleaned, and the administrator is done talking to Mr. Corrigan.

JULIA. How long will that be?

RAYMOND. A while. I'm sure he has a lot of things to say. Where's your friend? How long can it take him to change clothes?

JULIA. Kevin? *(calling out the door)* Kevin? There you are, we'll be in here until your clothes are dry. The Laundry lady said she was running a load through, anyway, so it shouldn't be long. Come in.

KEVIN'S VOICE. *(off)* I feel silly.

JULIA. You don't look silly. *(KEVIN scoffs at this.)* Kevin, Nurse Raymond promised to turn the heat up. *(to RAYMOND:)* I don't know about you, but I live in fear of bare thighs on cold vinyl. *(to KEVIN:)* Please come in.

KEVIN'S VOICE. I look stupid.

RAYMOND. Well, you can't stay out there dressed like that—someone's bound to come along and take blood.

(KEVIN enters in a striped hospital gown. It is flourescently

striped, and barely reaches to his knees. He is self-conscious and not happy.)

RAYMOND. Don't be upset. You were lucky 4 East could loan us a gown. *(to JULIA:)* I'll be back as soon as the Administrator is done. *(to KEVIN:)* When your clothes are dry, I'll bring them in.

KEVIN. When will that be?

RAYMOND. Am I a washing machine?

JULIA. Please don't snap at Kevin, Nurse Raymond. Its not his fault you're wet.

RAYMOND. And whose fault is it? Yours or Corrigan's?

JULIA. I wasn't involved.

RAYMOND. You *were* involved. I'm not stupid, Mrs. Muir, your boyfriend-roommate pulls whatever stunts he can think of—

JULIA. *(timidly)* He's not my boyfriend—

RAYMOND. And then sends ward princess in to smooth out any trouble. I won't have it anymore!

KEVIN. Don't talk to her like that. *(She looks at him.)* Please.

RAYMOND. How should I talk to her? Should I have to put up with this? *(to JULIA:)* Do you know what it feels like to have piss all over you?

KEVIN. *(with thought)* Yes.

RAYMOND. What do I do to deserve this? I minister to the sick is what I do. You'd think I'd be treated with a little respect—

JULIA. *(gently)* Nurse Raymond? You're dripping.

RAYMOND. I know that! *(suddenly uncomfortable with her*

clothes) I'm going to change. Now, behave yourself for once. *(To herself as she leaves.)* God, I hate this.

KEVIN. That woman is a—

JULIA. *(helpfully)* Bitch?

KEVIN. Thank you. Something should be done about her.

JULIA. *(excited)* Are you going to tell her off?

KEVIN. I'd like to.

JULIA. Can I watch?

KEVIN. I can't, Julia, it's not my place. She's not the problem, anyway. He is.

JULIA. Who is?

KEVIN. Jack! That madman ought to be locked up!

JULIA. *(tentatively)* He's not that bad—

KEVIN. Oh, come on, Julia. You can't approve of the way he treats people. And then you get blamed for the things he does. *(pause)* You ought to move to another room.

JULIA. He has his good points—

KEVIN. Rasputin had his good points, but I wouldn't share a room with him. Don't you see they put you in with him because you're too sweet to complain?

JULIA. You think I'm sweet, huh?

KEVIN. You never complain, Julia. You always see the positive side. *(Pause, more to himself.)* I admire that, I really do. *(pause)*

JULIA. *(curious)* Kevin, you're early this week.

KEVIN. *(more distantly)* I had some time...

JULIA. Why?

KEVIN. *(suddenly)* I'm serious about that room change, though. You shouldn't—

JULIA. Kevin, why are you here on a Monday? *(pause)*

KEVIN. *(energetic)* I'm going back to Law School, Julia. It's something I never gave a fair try.

JULIA. Is that what you want?

KEVIN. It's a smart career move, I think. A more secure future. *(Crosses away from her, to the window.)* I think you can see the Law School from here.

JULIA. Would you be happy?

KEVIN. I think so.

JULIA. And so would your mother? *(KEVIN looks at her.)*

KEVIN. Yeah, so I gave some thought to what she said. Did it occur to you that I might be happier as a lawyer?

JULIA. You're happy as a teacher, though.

KEVIN. Teaching is a waste of time. The facilities around here are fair, at best. The kids are a nightmare...

JULIA. But you're good at it. *(pause)*

KEVIN. Yeah, but the school has this new incentive program to get me back into Law School.

JULIA. What do you mean?

KEVIN. They laid me off. *(She starts to speak.)* Don't get excited. It's not as bad as it sounds. I was pink-slipped, effective January, or pending a millage increase.

JULIA. What does that mean?

KEVIN. It means they laid me off. I'm sorry, Julia. Maybe it's best. This could be someone telling me to wake up, find something more secure...I've been trying to see it that way...

JULIA. But you don't feel that way?

KEVIN. I don't know, I...

JULIA. Tell me.

KEVIN. *(with great intimacy)* I feel—

(ORDERLY bursts in through the door, carrying a bucket and mop. He sees only the floor and JULIA.)

ORDERLY. *(to JULIA)* I'm supposed to clean up in here. *(He looks at the puddle left by RAYMOND.)* Right here. *(He starts mopping.)*

JULIA. *(uncomfortably)* Now? Could you possibly do my room first?

ORDERLY. 412? *(SHE nods.)* Cleaned it. The hallway, too. *(Smiles. Mops.)*

JULIA. Thank you, Jeff.

ORDERLY. *(As HE finishes.)* Some accident, huh? He should have used a urinal.

KEVIN. *(to himself)* He did.

JULIA. *(to the ORDERLY)* It wasn't Jack.

KEVIN. *(to JULIA)* And it wasn't an accident. *(ORDERLY sees KEVIN for the first time.)*

ORDERLY. *(Grabbing KEVIN and ushering him to the door.)* Okay, buddy, you're out of bounds. Back to 4 East.

JULIA. You can't do that, Jeff.

ORDERLY. Senility patients shouldn't wander off 4 East. They'll hurt themselves.

KEVIN. I'm not a senility patient.

ORDERLY. Yes, you are.

JULIA. No, he's not.

ORDERLY. I've seen him here before.

JULIA. He's just visiting.

ORDERLY. *(Tapping his temple.) That's* why he belongs on 4 East. *(starts to go)*

JULIA. Wait.

ORDERLY. I'm sorry, Mrs. Muir. It's my job.

JULIA. Does he *look* like a senility patient?

KEVIN. I don't think so.

ORDERLY. *(to KEVIN)* You stay out of this. *(To JULIA, as he touches KEVIN'S gown.)* He's got this on, doesn't he?

KEVIN. *(To the ORDERLY, earnestly:)* My clothes are covered with urine.

ORDERLY. *(to JULIA)* See?

JULIA. Jeff, he's my regular Thursday visitor. He's wearing the gown until his clothes are clean. *(pause)* Really.

ORDERLY. *(to JULIA)* Then I got one question. *(to KEVIN)* You always piss down hallways? Who taught you hygiene, junior?

KEVIN. I didn't piss in the hallway.

ORDERLY. Well, somebody did, and somebody tracked it in here. And I want to know who!

JULIA. Nurse Raymond. *(Pause. HE turns, looks at her, looks at the floor, looks at her.)*

ORDERLY. Naaaah. *(JULIA nods.)* Really?

JULIA. She was just in here.

ORDERLY. *(Picking up the mop and bucket, with dread.)* Where else did she...go?

JULIA. She went to get changed. Stay away from her, though. She's very upset. *(HE looks with disdain at the mop head.)*

ORDERLY. Upset? She would have to be. *(HE leaves.)*

JULIA. Kevin, I'm sorry.

KEVIN. *(smiling)* It's alright. At least it got my mind off things.

JULIA. Like losing your job?

KEVIN. Yeah, like that.

JULIA. You know, I think we've been looking at this the wrong way. *(KEVIN looks at her.)* You're free, Kevin. No...think about it. You have the chance to explore anything with your life now. New jobs, new experiences...I think this was meant to be.

KEVIN. Destiny again.

JULIA. Maybe.

KEVIN. Suppose all I ever wanted was to teach? I was pretty good at that job, Julia, and no amount of freedom is going to make me miss it less.

JULIA. Is teaching what you want? *(KEVIN nods.)* Then go out and teach.

KEVIN. No amount of hoping is going to get that millage increase.

JULIA. So?

KEVIN. That means I'll have to go to another school district.

JULIA. *(energetically)* So, go!

KEVIN. That means I'll have to move. *(Pause. JULIA crosses to the window.)* Julia—

JULIA. *(quiet, but determined)* Then go. For you. There's nothing tying you down.

KEVIN. Yes there is.

JULIA. Kevin, I know your mother would not want you to stay here for Law School.

KEVIN. It's not Law School.

JULIA. A person lives their whole life, Kevin, and one day they are gone and there is nothing to say they were ever there. Nothing. Except the people who carry on in their name; touching, helping other people, and so on...maybe that's the only thing that matters. I don't know. All I know is, if you tie yourself here, and live your life as an apology to someone else, it all stops. And you stop. I don't think anyone would want that.

KEVIN. Some people are worth the risk.

JULIA. Your mother is dead, Kevin—

KEVIN. I didn't mean my mother, I meant you. *(silence)*

JULIA. *(backing up)* That would be worse! No! My life is fine, Kevin! I don't complain! I never said you had to come here!

KEVIN. I never came because I had to. Julia? Calm down!

JULIA. *(not hearing him)* Don't think of me like that!

KEVIN. I don't!

JULIA. Then why did you say that?

KEVIN. I don't know!

JULIA. I wouldn't tie you down, Kevin! At...arm's length from the world—!

KEVIN. *(trying to calm her)* I believe you—

JULIA. The whole world, Kevin! Think of that! Everything on the other side of this window—all the things I can't touch—*that's* what I want for you...you have your youth... *(SHE is getting winded, and slowing down.)* ...your freedom.

KEVIN. Freedom is one scary word.

JULIA. Some of the finest things in life are scary.

KEVIN. You're right. *(HE thinks, laughs, starts walking*

around. JULIA is left at the window.) I've been using you as an excuse. *(JULIA looks at the ground.)* This *could* be an opportunity I never—I mean, I like it here, but I could be happy somewhere else. I could be *needed* someplace else...

JULIA. *(distantly)* I have enough. I don't complain. *(KEVIN looks at her. Shrugs it off.)*

KEVIN. *(to himself)* It's a lot to think about.

JULIA. Nobody owes anybody.

KEVIN. What?

JULIA. Nobody owes anybody, Jack!

KEVIN. Kevin.

JULIA. Kevin, I'm sorry. *(pause)*

KEVIN. *(laugh)* How could you confuse us? I'm tall, gorgeous, and candy-striped. Jack's short, dark and obscene. *(pause)* Ha ha. *(pause)* Julia?

JULIA. *(suddenly)* I told him he doesn't owe me. That's not why he comes! *(SHE stands.)*

KEVIN. Told who? *(steps toward her)*

JULIA. *(distantly)* I'm tired of being careful, Jack. *(angrily)* I'm tired of being careful!

KEVIN. Julia?

JULIA. *(confused)* Kevin? *(HE nods, SHE smiles, gestures by her shoulder.)* I was just telling Jack here... *(HE takes her gently by the arm.)*

KEVIN. Julia, let's sit you down. *(He helps her to a chair.)*

JULIA. It's not ugly here, is it, Kevin?

KEVIN. *(Gently, trying to look into her eyes.)* No, Julia, it isn't, no.

JULIA. *(Looking squarely at KEVIN.)* It must be the way

we *see* it, Jack. We mustn't scare them with what we see. *(pause)* I feel sick.

KEVIN. *(rising)* I'm going to get someone.

JULIA. Kevin?

KEVIN. It's alright, Julia. I'm getting a nurse. *(She looks around, curiously.)*

JULIA. Did I faint?

KEVIN. You don't remember?

JULIA. We were talking about Law School. *(alarmed)* Nothing happened, did it?

KEVIN. No. You just said you were tired, so I was getting a nurse.

JULIA. Oh, good. I didn't want to scare you, is all.

KEVIN. Oh no. *(Opening the door, calling.)* Hey! Can we get a nurse down here? *(closes the door)*

JULIA. You can't make your life an apology to her.

KEVIN. *(carefully)* What are you talking about, Julia?

JULIA. Law School, silly. *(SHE laughs, HE laughs, relieved.)*

KEVIN. Oh, yeah, I forgot.

JULIA. You have trouble keeping your mind on things.

KEVIN. *(smiles)* Yeah, I'm terrible that way.

(Enter RAYMOND.)

RAYMOND. What's wrong?

KEVIN. Nothing. She's just tired and wants to go to bed.

RAYMOND. *(calling outside)* Jeff? I need you to take Mrs. Muir to her room. *(to JULIA)* Are you alright, Mrs. Muir?

JULIA. Oh, yes. Just a little winded.

(Enter ORDERLY.)

JULIA. And you? Are you drier now?

RAYMOND. Yes. *(ORDERLY takes JULIA gently by the arm.)*

KEVIN. *(to JULIA)* See you on Thursday?

JULIA. Oh, yes? *(HE nods.)* Oh—twice this week! Oh, good. I'm glad you're feeling better, Mrs. Raymond.

RAYMOND. Thank you.

JULIA. And I'm sure you'll get used to Jack, in time.

RAYMOND. Let's not talk about it, I'll just get upset.

ORDERLY. *(As HE takes JULIA out.)* Oh, God, no. *(THEY are gone. RAYMOND gives KEVIN his clean clothes. HE puts them on.)*

KEVIN. Sometimes I forget...she's old.

RAYMOND. That's why we keep an eye on them, and why we have rules.

KEVIN. I worry about her.

RAYMOND. Sharing a room with him isn't helping any. It's way too much excitement.

KEVIN. I'll take care of that. Thank you.

RAYMOND. That would solve a lot of problems. Because I know she encourages him to make trouble when they're together. *(KEVIN finishes dressing, hands her the gown.)*

KEVIN. Nurse Raymond?

RAYMOND. Yes?

KEVIN. Don't be such a bitch. *(HE exits. SHE watches him go, shakes her head, and exits.)*

BLACKOUT

SCENE TWO

JACK and JULIA'S room, immediately afterward. JACK is sitting near the window in a wheelchair. The room is dark. JULIA enters.

JULIA. Jack? Is everybody gone?

JACK. *(softly)* They had at me and left. Fuck 'em. *(loudly)* Fuck 'em!

JULIA. Ssssh. What did they say? *(During the following, SHE pulls up her chair next to JACK, SHE retrieves the cigarettes from the secret place in his bed, and sits next to him.)*

JACK. What could they say? What could they do? Send me to prison? *(Laughs, a bit forced, looks around the room.)* There's nothing they could do under the heading of "punishment" that they don't already do under the heading of "therapy."

JULIA. They were angry, weren't they?

JACK. Angry..."Go ahead and beat me," I said, "word'll get out: Nursing Home Cruelty—Geriatrics piss in formation. Film at eleven." They said what I did was psychotically cruel. *(laughs)* "Psychotically cruel"—it wasn't psychotically cruel...was it?

JULIA. It was cruel.

JACK. No, it wasn't!

JULIA. Yes, it was.

JACK. No, it wasn't...it might have been psychotic, but it sure as hell wasn't cruel...what *she* did to *me*...oh, fuck.

Never mind... *(She hands him a cigarette and lighter. He lights it, smokes.)*

JULIA. You're not psychotic, Jack.

JACK. I know that! *(Pause)* I'm psycho*path*ic, but I like to think I bring it off with style.

JULIA. If you were psychotic, I wouldn't stay with you.

JACK. Oh, bullshit! You'd sit naked on a cactus and sing if anyone asked you to. You have no taste. *(She takes the cigarette from him.)*

JULIA. No one made me stay with you. *(SHE inhales, coughs.)*

JACK. I know... *(Silence. HE takes the cigarette back.)* As I said, no taste.

JULIA. You know why I moved in here?

JACK. Yeah, I know, you don't have to go into it.

JULIA. Because you have spirit.

JACK. Yeah, yeah—

JULIA. An unbreakable spirit. *(silence)* Do you remember when I met you? They wheeled you by while I was in the hallway?

JACK. *(reluctantly)* And that...that candy-striper was trying to hook up your IV.

JULIA. And she couldn't find the vein, and she kept trying and I was crying. And you refused to leave until she got someone else. You started screaming and they were trying to shut you up. Do you remember what you said? "Spirit is all I got. My legs may shut down, my arms may shut down. But my spirit will fight while my body retires..."

JACK. *(quietly)* "Through my mouth, while it works..."

JULIA. "Through my eyes, while I see, through my mind while I think. You can never break my spirit..."

JACK. *(softly)* I was pretty eloquent that day... *(pause)*

JULIA. Jack, were you crying?

JACK. *(not hearing)* You would have been proud of my spirit today, Julia.

JULIA. Would I?

JACK. They told me to apologize. I said, "You make *her* apologize." Then they said she could sue me. I said. "For what? My gallstones? I'll settle out of court right here and now." Then they said they could put me on sedatives. I told them, "I'll spit anything you give me right back in your face. From either oriface." *(SHE laughs.)* Then they said they could move you to another part of the ward. *(silence)*

JULIA. And what did you do? *(pause)*

JACK. Then I apologized. *(SHE touches a tear on his face. HE laughs.)* Really put on an act for 'em, too. Ass-holes.

JULIA. Thank you.

JACK. For what?

JULIA. Protecting me.

JACK. I wasn't...well, yeah, well, you're welcome.

JULIA. *(Gets up, wheels him to his bed.)* I'm not moving anywhere.

JACK. I know that, stupid! Didn't I just see to that? God!

JULIA. *(As JACK gets in bed.)* Thank you.

JACK. And don't thank me. I do what *I* want. *(She starts to leave.)* You going?

JULIA. For now.

JACK. How's the Prince of Kidney? Still pretty ripe?

JULIA. He's cleaned up.

JACK. I didn't mean it for him, you know.

JULIA. I know.

JACK. Too bad. *(reluctantly)* I was almost thinking of tagging along to harass you two today.

JULIA. You should have! *(Distantly, HE shakes his head.)*

JACK. Don't take too long. *(quickly)* I short-sheeted your bed. I want to be awake for your reaction.

JULIA. I won't. *(She closes the door. He lies back in the bed. LIGHTS FADE.)*

BLACKOUT

SCENE THREE

The Solarium, the next day. ORDERLY is mopping, enter SUTTON and RAYMOND from the hall.

RAYMOND. I don't want to talk about it.

SUTTON. Well, I think we should. You're not used to this floor, Pat, you have to understand some things—

RAYMOND. No. I have been a charge nurse for a long time, Ms. Sutton, and a damn good one, too. If I am...degraded, I won't sit idly by and try to understand it. *(During the following, SUTTON and RAYMOND bring their conversation away from the ORDERLY and towards the window.*

ORDERLY, in an effort to eavesdrop, mops close on their heels, less and less discreetly.)

SUTTON. Then you should know they feel the same way. Mr. Corrigan is still very sharp, very aware. If he feels he can use a bathroom, why not let him use the bathroom?

RAYMOND. That is not what his chart says. You stick to the chart because *that* is what's best—whether they realize it or not. You let them do whatever they want, and you may seem like the good guy—but one day they will hurt themselves and *then* who's to blame?

SUTTON. Alright. On this shift, let *me* take care of 412. You lay off, and things will calm down.

RAYMOND. *(protesting)* If I hear any ruckus—

SUTTON. You won't. *(ORDERLY drops his bucket noisely. BOTH look at him. HE smiles. BOTH look at him. HE backs away. To RAYMOND.)* You won't. Mr. Corrigan and Mrs. Muir will be as quiet as mice. I promise. *(pause)*

RAYMOND. You're only asking for trouble. Indulging them like that. *(exits)*

SUTTON. I'll take that chance. *(exits)*

(LIGHTS CROSSFADE to JACK and JULIA'S room.)

SCENE FOUR

JACK and JULIA'S room, a few minutes later. During the change, JACK has moved a nightstand table over to block the door. HE watches television and smokes while JULIA is in the bathroom. Knock at the door.

JACK. *(Crushing out the cigarette and wielding the can from his bed.)* You get the fuck out of here, you bitch, or I'll break both your knees!

SUTTON. *(from outside)* What's blocking this door?

(JULIA comes out of the bathroom.)

JULIA. Jack, you blocked the door?

JACK. I mean it! I got hostages in here. I got an old lady!

JULIA. Thank you.

JACK. And I don't care who I hurt!

JULIA. You wouldn't hurt me.

JACK. *(to her, urgently)* It's a bluff, dammit, what do you care? *(to door)* So, back off!

JULIA. Jack, that's Nurse Sutton.

JACK. No it's not.

SUTTON. *(from outside)* Yes it is.

JACK. No, it's not. That's not Sutton's voice. That's old boulder-butt trying to trick me.

SUTTON. Who caught you watching *The Young and the Restless* last Wednesday?

JACK. *(after a pause)* Sutton? Are you alone?

SUTTON. Yes, I am, but I can get Nurse Raymond if you want more company.

JACK. Let her in, will you?

JULIA. You told me you hate *The Young and the Restless*—

JACK. *(impatiently)* Will you just let her in?

(SHE goes to the door, inches the night table away. SUTTON comes in, not pleased.)

JACK. What do you want?

SUTTON. I want— *(Abruptly SHE stops, steps away and checks the doorway for urinals, as she replaces the night table.)* I want to run a decent, efficient floor here, and that is something I can't do with you barricading the door. Now, I know you're afraid of Nurse Raymond—

JACK. I most certainly am not afraid of her—

SUTTON. Then why are you blocking the door, Mr. C.? *(She goes to get water from the bathroom to give him his pill.)* Suppose you had a stroke or something and no one could get in because the door was blocked?

JACK. The quality of my medical care would dramatically increase.

SUTTON: *(to JULIA)* Talk to him please, will you? *(As SHE goes in the bathroom.)* I had a talk with Raymond. As long as you keep your nose clean and stick to your chart, the only one coming in here will be me. *(SHE comes out, gives him a pill and water, which SHE watches him take.)* But the first infraction—and I mean the smallest thing—and she'll be in here again to read you the riot act, clear?

JULIA. *(for JACK)* Clear.

SUTTON. *(As SHE puts back the glass and writes in his chart.)* Now that means rest, no television between one and four. *(turns off TV)* and no excess noise. And, please, use the urinal. *As* a urinal—not a projectile. *(writes)* Any questions?

JACK. *(raising his hand)* Why are you such a bitch today?

SUTTON. *(putting down the chart)* Because I caught a lot of flak for what happened yesterday, and I wasn't even here! And—much as I dislike her personally—it *galls* me to have another nurse treated that way. *(starting to leave, facing the door)* And...if you *had* to do something that terrible, you could at least have waited until I was here to see it! *(exits)*

JACK. I've started a spectator sport.

JULIA. That doesn't mean she approves of what you did.

JACK. Oh, for God's sakes, Julia—face it. The woman was asking for it. It was destiny. Somewhere there is a bedpan with her name on it.

(Knock at door. JACK grabs the cane.)

JACK. Who is it?

SUTTON. *(off)* Proctology.

JACK. That's not funny.

(As SUTTON enters.)

SUTTON. I forgot what I came in here for in the first

place. *(to JULIA)* You have a visitor in the Solarium.

JULIA. *(rising quickly)* Oh, alright, I'll be right there.

JACK. Who is it? *(She shrugs.)* He was here yesterday. How often does that wimp need his nose wiped?

JULIA. About as often as we all do. What makes you think it's him?

JACK. Who the hell else could it be? You don't socialize that much. Do you?

JULIA. I prefer to remain a woman of mystery. *(SUTTON laughs. JULIA exits.)*

JACK. *(calling after her)* Woman of mystery, my ass. I know every varicose vein you got! *(SUTTON shoots him a cross look.)* Oh, come on, that wasn't loud. I'm not even up to full voice yet.

SUTTON. *(drawing up a chair)* I think we should have a talk.

(CROSSFADE to Solarium, KEVIN reads a magazine, stands as JULIA enters.)

JULIA. Kevin! How nice of you to come! *(hugs him)*

KEVIN. You called me.

JULIA. Oh. Yes, but it was nice of you to oblige, don't you think?

KEVIN. The message on my service sounded so urgent, I couldn't very well stay away. Now, what's wrong?

JULIA. Nothing with me, thank God. But I need a favor.

KEVIN. Anything.

JULIA. Do you know what your friendship has done for me?

KEVIN. *(confused)* ...yes.

JULIA. What?

KEVIN. ...I don't know. What do you think?

JULIA. I think you know.

KEVIN. Is this the favor? Do you want me to write it down or something? *(pause)* I give you—we give each other—someone...to look forward to...is this right?

JULIA. Exactly. And it has done wonders for me.

KEVIN. Likewise.

JULIA. And last night I discovered someone who is starving for a relationship like ours. A little of your companionship could help.

KEVIN. *(flattered)* Oh...well...a friend of yours is a friend of mine. You say you met last night?

JULIA. Actually we've known each other for some time, but last night was the first time I saw this...tender little person inside, screaming for companionship. Can you imagine?

KEVIN. I think so. Sure, I'd like to help. *(She takes his arm.)*

JULIA. Thank you so much. You are so generous, Kevin. And brave.

KEVIN. Well, I'm working on that...why brave?

JULIA. Hmmm?

KEVIN. Why brave? Why is it brave to help this "tender little person?" *(pause)*

JULIA. Because he's trapped inside Jack.

KEVIN. *(crossing away)* Oh, God.

JULIA. Kevin, please—

KEVIN. Julia, he hates my guts.

JULIA. He needs some one.

KEVIN. Yeah, someone with a straight jacket. He yells and screams whenever he sees me, you know that.

JULIA. For me?

KEVIN. Look, if there is a little person inside, he's dammed little and well-hidden, and if he's so tender he's probably dead by now, anyway. Want to get a Coke?

JULIA. Why won't you do me this favor?

KEVIN. Because it won't work, Julia. He *hates* me.

JULIA. He doesn't hate you—he just doesn't know you.

KEVIN. Fine. He'll know me, *then* he'll hate me.

JULIA. You're underestimating your powers of charm.

KEVIN. And you're overestimating *his* powers of civility. Julia, I wore the man's urinal as a hat.

JULIA. You don't have to be afraid of him while I'm there.

KEVIN. Wait, wait! Who said I was afraid? *(laughs)* I'm not afraid.

JULIA. Then why won't you see him?

KEVIN. It wouldn't work. We have nothing in common.

JULIA. *We* have nothing in common.

KEVIN. Yes, *we* do—*we're* both human beings.

JULIA. Now you're being unfair. *(HE starts to speak.)* Kevin, you're very decent, and you've given me a lot of reasons why you refuse to see him. Jack, in all his indecency, hasn't refused to see you. *(pause)* I know he's been bad to you, and you have good cause to hold a grudge...It was just a thought I had last night...Maybe it is a little silly. I can't hold it against you if you don't want to. Sorry to drag you down here on a wild goose chase. *(pause)*

KEVIN. You want a Coke?

JULIA. Hmmmm?

KEVIN. I'm going to the cafeteria to think about it. You want a Coke?

JULIA. *(pleased)* No, thank you. *(pause)*

KEVIN. You'd have to go through the doorway first.

JULIA. I understand that.

KEVIN. Well...I'll *think* about it.

(CROSSFADE back to JACK'S room as SUTTON leaves. JACK turns on the TV, lights a cigarette. Knocking at the door.)

JACK. You stay the hell away—! *(JULIA comes in.)* You could at least let me finish my threats.

JULIA. *(giddy)* I don't have time. I have a surprise.

JACK. You're pregnant.

JULIA. No.

JACK. That *is* a surprise.

JULIA. I brought a surprise for you.

JACK. You dear girl. You brought me Raymond's head on a stick.

JULIA. Better. I brought you a visitor.

JACK. Don't be silly. No one wants to see me. Alive, anyway.

JULIA. You're wrong. I brought somebody who asked to see you.

JACK. Bullshit.

JULIA. They're right outside. *(pause)* Are you curious?

JACK. No! *(pause)* Let 'em in...

JULIA. First say, "Thank you, Julia, for bringing me

this good news."

JACK. Fuck you.

JULIA. Close enough. *(calling)* Ta-da! *(No response, SHE crosses to the door, swings it open.)* Ta-da!

(KEVIN enters sullenly, after checking the doorway for urinals. Pause JACK and KEVIN look at each other blankly.)

KEVIN. *(dully)* Hi. *(pause)*

JACK. *(to JULIA)* What the hell is this?

JULIA. It's your visitor.

JACK. No, it's one of *your* used-up visitors you're giving to me second-hand.

JULIA. *(whispering, to JACK)* He asked to see you, now *talk* to him. *(JACK clears his throat loudly, turns his attention to KEVIN, staring at him. Pause.)*

KEVIN. Hi.

JACK. *(to JULIA)* I want a *fresh* visitor. *(JULIA gestures, "talk to him.")* Why are you here?

KEVIN. To see you.

JACK. *(to JULIA)* Oooh, mind like a steel trap. *(to KEVIN)* Well, you've seen me, you can go. *(KEVIN looks at JULIA, then starts to leave. To JULIA)* How'd you get him to do this? Beg him or pay him?

JULIA. Neither.

KEVIN. She bet me that you could be civil to me for five minutes.

JULIA. *(getting the idea)* That's right! Pay you on Thursday, Kevin.

JACK. Wait. Wait. Wait. Wait. Wait. Come back here. *(HE does. JULIA smiles.)* You didn't tell me it was a profit deal. *(to JULIA)* Is the meter running? *(JULIA thinks for a moment, nods. To KEVIN.)* Do sit down. *(HE does.)* So. You're in this for the money, huh?

KEVIN. *(carefully)* Not just the money. I figured you were worth giving the benefit of the doubt.

JACK. Oh? And what about me convinced you of that?

KEVIN. You're breathing, aren't you?

JACK. Ooooh, clever, aren't we? *(Quoting Romeo & Juliet.)* "Thy wit is a-very bitter-sweeting; it is—"

JACK and KEVIN. "—a most sharp sauce."

KEVIN. *Romeo and Juliet.*

JACK. Act three—

KEVIN. Two, scene—

JACK. Four.

JULIA. Oooh, isn't this neat? *(Both look at JULIA.)*

JACK. *(to KEVIN)* Annoying sometimes, isn't she?

KEVIN. No.

JULIA. *(earnestly)* Oh, yes I am! Sometimes!

KEVIN. *(little laugh)* Okay, she is, sometimes.

JACK. *(to JULIA)* That's amazing, you know, I never see your lips move.

JULIA. Jack, please be nice.

JACK. Excuse me?

JULIA. Please be nice. Kevin is making an effort to converse with you.

JACK. Julia, are you telling me how to conduct myself with *my* guests?

JULIA. After all the unpleasantness of the last few days, wouldn't it be nice to have a few more people on our side?

JACK. It would be nice. *(looking at KEVIN)* It wouldn't be likely.

JULIA. *(moving toward JACK)* Maybe if you tried talking to him—

JACK. I'm talking! Don't you see me talking?

KEVIN. Maybe if you tried talking *to* me. I'm sorry to interrupt, but is it so hard to talk *to* someone? *(no response)* I think I'm a fairly easy person to talk to.

JACK. Why is that, do you think?

KEVIN. *(shrugs)* I don't know.

JACK. *(mimicking)* I dunno. Yes you do. You think you're some shit-hot Ann Landers-type and you have precise reason why.

KEVIN. I'm a good listener, I guess. People feel comfortable around me. *(looks to JULIA)* They seem to be able to let their feelings out more easily around me—

JACK. Than around me?

KEVIN. I didn't say that, no.

JACK. Well, it's true, isn't it? I think it's true, and do you know why? *(pause)* Because I consider you a sensitive person. *(to JULIA)* Don't you?

JULIA. Kevin is a very sensitive person.

JACK. Sensitive to you, sensitive to me, sensitive to himself...I admire that.

KEVIN. You don't sound like it.

JACK. *(Quoting Byron.)* "What is the worst of woes that wait on age? What stamps the wrinkle deeper on the brow—" *(to KEVIN)* Do you know it? *(KEVIN shakes his head.)* "—to view each loved one blotted from life's page, And be alone on earth, as I am now."

KEVIN. No one has to be alone.

JACK. And yet so many people are. Why do you suppose that is? With so many sensitive people like yourself, willing to attach themselves to cantankerous old farts like us?

KEVIN. I don't know.

JACK. Yes you do.

KEVIN. *(smiling)* Yes I do, but my answer isn't nearly as articulate as yours. *(both laugh)*

JACK. You're right. I think it's because you get so much out of the gesture of helping—well, let's say Julia, here. Isn't that right?

JULIA. Yes.

KEVIN. Yes.

JACK. It's a rewarding gesture. As a matter of fact, it's *so* rewarding, that's all it is—is a gesture. Come once a week, listen to the old lady—!

JULIA. Jack! I won't have this!

JACK. *(continuing)* —don't get involved, just listen for awhile, and then you can pat yourself on the back for being a Boy Scout the rest of the week—

JULIA. Jack!

JACK. *(to her)* Sit down! I'm doing this for you! *(To KEVIN, as JACK rises.)* And then, once you accumulate enough points, you're free forever! Just stop showing up, isn't that the pattern? ISN'T IT?

KEVIN. It is for people who don't care! And...and for people who only want what they can get out of other people.

JACK. And what do you want out of her? A mother?

JULIA. Stop it! Please!

KEVIN. I have a friend! A good friendship, and I have

because I'm willing to trust people, and that's something you'll never be able to do.

JACK. Is that what you want? You want to be my friend? You want me to *trust* you?

JULIA. Kevin, I think you'd better go—

JACK. NO! Let him answer! Do you want me to trust you?

KEVIN. I was willing to give it a try. *(brief pause)*

JACK. That's big of you to give it a try while you rip Julia out of my life completely!

JULIA. What? Jack, what are you talking about?

JACK. Tell her! Tell her what Sutton told me this afternoon! *(to JULIA)* She told me I'd better shape up, because inquiries were made as to whether you could be moved to another part of the ward. And I don't have to think hard to guess who's making those inquiries!

JULIA. You're wrong, Jack. Kevin wouldn't do something like that—

KEVIN. Yes, he would. *(Silence, JULIA turns to him.)*

JULIA. Oh, Kevin, how could you move my room?

KEVIN. I just made some inquiries. I thought I could convince you. For your own good.

JACK. *(low)* For your own good. For your own fucking good. Isn't that always the case? They don't ask you, they don't even *think* about what you want—but they act on your behalf for your own good. Because you wouldn't know any better. No, you're old and you can't see or move so well so they think you don't *feel* anymore! Well, I feel! And I hurt, too, mister, and I'm not going to give a *lick* of that up in the name of your precious trust! And the day you take away the person I love is the day *after* I'm dead! *(Raising his cane to KEVIN.)* Now I want you out—!

JULIA. *(As JACK approaches KEVIN with the cane.)* Jack, he didn't mean to hurt you. Please give him a chance to explain—

JACK. NOW! Before I bash your useless head!

JULIA. Kevin, no! Don't leave me! Jack, please...I'm begging you to sit down before you hurt yourself.

JACK. GO!

KEVIN. *(tentatively)* Julia— *(JACK swings the cane—a warning strike—which KEVIN evades easily. JULIA screams.)* Now just calm down—

JACK. Go-away!

KEVIN. *(calmly)* I will, I will. Just settle down. Relax, and...I'll leave. *(gently)* I promise. I promise... *(JACK, exhausted, slumps on the edge of the bed and lets the cane drop. KEVIN gently removes it and places it alongside JACK'S bed. He looks at JULIA, to reassure her, and then to JACK, still hyperventilating, as KEVIN heads for the door.)* Okay?

JACK. *(softly)* Okay...

(With a quiet nod to JULIA, KEVIN opens the door to leave as RAYMOND comes in.)

RAYMOND. Corrigan, you have raised hell just once too often. *(She ushers JACK, unresisting, back on the bed during the following.)*

JULIA. It's alright now, Mrs. Raymond, everything's fine.

RAYMOND. The hell it is. You think I don't have ears? I won't have maniacs yelling on my floor and threatening people. *(to JACK)* We are going to get some sedatives from the pharmacy, and if I have any say in the matter, you're going to be out of here and in restraints. *(She raises the gates on each side of the bed.)*

JULIA. *(frightened)* Mrs. Raymond, that won't be necessary. He just got a little excited. He's fine now, just leave him alone.

RAYMOND. You be quiet. You're as bad as he is. You encourage him. *(She hunts for the bed straps.)*

KEVIN. We just had a little squabble here. We appreciate your concern, but it won't happen again.

RAYMOND. You're damn right it won't happen again. I'm through indulging you people. *(to JACK)* You are going to learn, my friend, that if you act like an animal, you're going to be treated like one. *(During the following, she weakly straps JACK'S arms in, and interrupts tightening the straps to deal with JULIA.)*

JULIA. *(crossing to her, angrily)* Don't you talk to him like that! You have no right to bully people—I don't care what kind of authority you have!

KEVIN. *(reaching for her)* Julia, stay out of this—

JULIA. *(brushing him aside)* Have you ever thought that maybe he's like this because of the way you treat him? You people, with your rules and your schedules, do you have to dictate everything? He's angry now, can you let him feel something without putting it under a microscope? *(RAYMOND leans JACK back on the bed, crossing down to strap his feet. JULIA grabs RAYMOND.)* LEAVE HIM ALONE! *(RAYMOND turns, seizes JULIA, slapping her once on the face and pushing her back toward KEVIN. JACK, regaining his breath watches this.)*

RAYMOND. YOU STAY BACK OR YOU'LL BE NEXT, UNDERSTAND? *(KEVIN pulls JULIA away, trying to comfort her. As RAYMOND turns back to tighten JACK'S armstraps, JACK touches her face gently, and speaks softly. Almost an invocation:)*

JACK. "Do Not Go Gentle Into That Good Night"*

RAYMOND. *(perfunctorily)* What? *(JACK'S vigor and tone increase during the following;)*

JACK. "Do not go gentle into that good night,
Old age should burn and rave at close of day;
Rage against the dying of the light."
(JACK has freed his right arm, waving it about as RAYMOND tries to put it in the strap.)
"Though wise men at their end know dark is right,
Because their words had forked no lightning they
Do not go gentle into that good night."
(JACK finds his cane, and wields it as a weapon at RAYMOND, who, surprised, backs away.)
"Good men, the last wave by, crying how bright
Their frail deeds might have danced in a green bay,
Rage, rage against the dying of the light."
(RAYMOND tries to persuade JACK to relinquish the cane.)
"Wild men who caught and sang the sun in flight,
And learn, too late, they grieved it on its way,
Do not go gentle into that good night."
(During this, RAYMOND can make a move for the cane, which JACK wards off with a swing. He should hold her trapped in the

**Do Not Go Gentle Into That Good Night,* by Dylan Thomas, used by permission of New Directions Publishing Co., New York, NY.

room until the final stanza, when she can slip by him, and out the door.)

"Grave men, near death, who see with blinding sight
Blind eyes could blaze like meteors and be gay,
Rage, rage against the dying of the light."

"And you, my father, there on the sad height,
Curse, bless, me now with your fierce tears, I pray.
Do not go gentle into that good night.
Rage, rage against the dying of the light."
(The final two lines should be to JULIA, as the lights dim.)

BLACK OUT

SCENE FIVE

Half-light in both Solarium and JACK and JULIA'S room. Hallway should be LIT FULL, or the hallway exchange can be done as voice-overs.

RAYMOND. *(turning over charts to MONTCRIEF)* Well, that's it. I'm going home.

MONTCRIEF. Rough day, huh?

RAYMOND. God, you don't know ... we had to wrestle him down and sedate him. We finally got him away, and Sutton's raising hell, and that kid — whoever he is. *(pause)* You know, people think I like to do this. I don't like to do this. But you gotta stick to the rules...

MONTCRIEF. ...Yeah.

RAYMOND. *(putting on her coat)* Okay, well—Oh. Wait. *(wearily)* I got to go in there again. I have to make sure Mrs. Muir isn't loose before I leave.

MONTCRIEF. I'll do it.

(Pause. Footsteps. JULIA appears in the Solarium one moment before MONTCRIEF goes to her room and finds her bed empty. MONTCRIEF looks around the room indecisively before RAYMOND calls from the hall.)

RAYMOND. Well? Is she there?

MONTCRIEF. *(from the room)* Yes. Yes she is, you can go home.

(RAYMOND, and MONTCRIEF exit. LIGHTS SLOWLY FADE on all but the Solarium. JULIA crosses to the window and, after a while, speaks to her imaginary friend. During the following, KEVIN slides in unnoticed.)

JULIA. It's quiet tonight, isn't it? It's always quiet after bad things happen. That's when you hear the quiet. *(laugh)* Honestly, there's so much screaming, and then...there's this quiet telling you it never really happened. But you remember. Sometimes remembering makes the noise even louder. *(pause)* Let's talk about something else, shall we? Are you from Michigan originally? I'm from California. The San Joaquin Valley—

KEVIN. *(gently)* You never told me about the San Joaquin Valley— *(JULIA starts.)*

JULIA. You frightened me.

KEVIN. I'm sorry.

JULIA. That's the thing about imaginary visitors. They never sneak up on you. *(pause)*

KEVIN. I'm sorry for what happened today, Julia. I didn't mean to go behind your back, I—

JULIA. They took him away, you know. They strapped him in and took him away. He wasn't fighting, either. He was just...staring at me.

KEVIN. I didn't know you two felt so strongly for each other.

JULIA. Neither did I. Isn't that a terrible thing to find out at the last minute? *(HE goes to comfort her. SHE moves away.)* Don't feel sorry for me.

KEVIN. I worry about you.

JULIA. I don't think you should come here anymore, Kevin.

KEVIN. Because I tried to move your room?

JULIA. Because it's best. Because you have a life to get on with. And so do I. And sooner or later...we lead very different lives, as you said.

KEVIN. I thought we were doing pretty well until today. I'm sorry about today, Julia.

JULIA. It's not your fault, it's mine. Jack told me this might happen. Who we are. Where we are...there are just too many ways to get hurt. I should have listened. It's not your fault. I will always treasure you, Kevin. I just have to let go now. *(gently)* Alright? *(He nods.)* Goodbye, Kevin.

KEVIN. Goodbye. *(Pause. She turns away. KEVIN does not move. JULIA looks at him.)*

JULIA. You're not moving.

KEVIN. Yeah, I noticed that.

JULIA. Do you want *me* to leave?

KEVIN. No. You stay. Please. *(pause)*

JULIA. Kevin, one of us has to leave, if we're saying goodbye.

KEVIN. I know. I just wanted to apologize.

JULIA. You have. Four times. You did what you thought was best, Kevin. You've been wonderful. This is my decision. *(pause)* Anything else?

KEVIN. Yes.

JULIA. What?

KEVIN. I'm sorry.

JULIA. *(angrily)* Will you listen to me?

KEVIN. I don't like losing friends.

JULIA. You're not! You're still my friend! You will always be my friend! I just...don't want to see you anymore.

KEVIN. That doesn't make sense. Why don't you—

JULIA. Because sooner or later you'd leave anyway! You'll want to leave! And you'll leave slow! Skip a Thursday, skip two, then just stop coming altogether—

KEVIN. You've been listening to Jack.

JULIA. *(flaring)* Don't you talk about Jack to me!

KEVIN. He's been scaring you!

JULIA. He's my friend—

KEVIN. So am I!

JULIA. *He* understands! He is someone I can scream to! He sees all the ugliness around, and can still care...

KEVIN. Julia, what are you talking about?

JULIA. You don't know! I've lied to keep from frightening you.

KEVIN. And whose fault is that?

JULIA. Yours! You can't afford to see past yourself—

KEVIN. Or you're afraid to trust me.

JULIA. *(laughs)* Oh yes, "trust me, tell me." That's what they all say. That's what Lorraine used to say—

KEVIN. Who is Lorraine?

JULIA. *(continuing)* —and so I did. I told her about loneliness; about being tied to machines, and probed and measured and treated like everything but a human being. I took her in here and I said, "God I hate this life!" *(pause)*

KEVIN. *(softly)* What happened?

JULIA. *(angrily)* Do you see her here? Do you hear the phone ring? Do you find any card, or word, or *mention* of her? "Trust me, tell me." Well, what I have to tell is too much!

KEVIN. So you lied.

JULIA. *(proudly)* About everything. I gave you a perfect, happy woman, Kevin. I gave you a dancer—

KEVIN. Because you just couldn't chance being honest—

JULIA. *(overlapping, angrily)* Because you couldn't take it! Old people are scary! They're frail, and they die! It's just too easy to head for the door and pretend they don't exist. Would you have visited me if I cried to you? Would you have cared for me if I wasn't "sweet?" Would you have given me a second look if I hadn't lied about your mother? *(Pause. KEVIN, somewhat shocked, walks away a few steps.)*

KEVIN. I guess we'll never know... *(pause)*

JULIA. I'm sorry you had to find out this way...but at least you'll leave knowing the truth.

KEVIN. What about you?

JULIA. I'll be fine.

KEVIN. That's not what I meant. What did you get out of all this? *(pause)*

JULIA. *(softly)* Please leave—

KEVIN. *(cutting her off)* Not until I get an answer!

JULIA. You couldn't understand—

KEVIN. Maybe not, but I deserve an explanation! I hear a whole lot about what *I* can't handle but you're the one running away! Why all the trouble, Julia?

JULIA. You couldn't—

KEVIN. Why all the fake stories and phony concern—

JULIA. It wasn't phony—

KEVIN. Why bother with a motherless school teacher at all—?

JULIA. Don't—

KEVIN. *Why?*

JULIA. *(finally)* Because I got a chance to help someone! To touch someone else's life, and feel I matter more than the pills they stick in me and the liquids they take out! ...I thought, if I could reach someone, I wouldn't feel like I died years ago...when people stopped seeing me... *(SHE cries.)* I'm sorry. I didn't mean to do this. I guess I'm getting sloppy in my old age. *(pause)* You have your answer...

KEVIN. Yes.

JULIA. You said you'd leave.

KEVIN. Yes. *(pause)*

JULIA. Goodbye.

KEVIN. Goodbye. *(Pause. Neither of them move.)*

JULIA. You're not leaving again.

KEVIN. Oh. Me? Oh, I thought *you* were leaving.

JULIA. It's my Solarium.

KEVIN. Ah. *(pause)*

JULIA. Aren't you going?

KEVIN. I can't. *(SHE looks at him.)* You're here.

JULIA. I—

KEVIN. That's what's amazing. *(SHE looks at him.)* The fact that you're here. And I'm here.

JULIA. *(smiling reluctantly)* We're both here.

KEVIN. I knew you'd understand! *(SHE crosses to him, hugs him.)* Destiny brought us together— *(SHE laughs a little.)* our paths were destined to cross, and a reason greater than ourselves has guided your path to me.

JULIA. The cafeteria was closed.

KEVIN. It was? Oh, what the hell—we'll improvise.

JULIA. *(carefully)* Are you going to come back?

KEVIN. Every Thursday.

JULIA. How can I believe that?

KEVIN. You'll just have to trust my solemn and sacred word as your friend.

JULIA. But—

KEVIN. Okay, here's my wallet. *(He gives it to her.)* And we're going to start talking about what a bitch you are, and how awful this place is.

JULIA. It isn't nice to hear.

KEVIN. It beats the hell out of Alaska. Can I say "hell" in front of you, now that you're not a "sweet little old lady?"

JULIA. *(tentatively)* If I can say "shit"...

KEVIN. Hell.

JULIA. Shit! Oh, that works fine! Jack should be here, we could give him lessons! *(She stops laughing.)*

KEVIN. You're worried about him, aren't you? *(SHE nods.)* Want me to wait with you? You can hide me from Ms. Montcrief—

JULIA. No, Kevin, thank you. Just now, I have to be alone with my thoughts. You can go, Kevin—

BOTH. 'til Thursday. *(SHE laughs.)*

KEVIN. Okay. *(HE kisses her gently on the head. Pause, and then:)* I love you...

JULIA. *(smiling)* I love you, too. *(HE smiles.)*

KEVIN. Meet you in the Solarium?

JULIA. *(an idea)* No, meet me in my room.

KEVIN. Won't Jack be there?

JULIA. I hope so. *(Pause. HE sighs.)*

KEVIN. Okay, meet you in your room. *(SHE tosses him his wallet. As HE leaves.)* I'll be the one wearing plastic.

(HE exits. SHE laughs. Slow fade on JULIA, alone.)

BLACKOUT

SCENE SIX

JACK and JULIA'S room, the next day. ORDERLY is in the room alone, singing to himself and collecting all of JULIA'S things. MONTCRIEF enters, Pause.

ORDERLY. Hi.

MONTCRIEF. Hi. *(MONTCRIEF looks at JULIA'S bed, reaches for the chart, which the ORDERLY gives her, and she starts filling it out.)*

ORDERLY. Are you speaking to me?

MONTCRIEF. Sounds like it.

ORDERLY. I'm sorry for what I did.

MONTCRIEF. *(little smile)* That's alright.

ORDERLY. Can I ask a question? What did I do?

MONTCRIEF. *(sigh)* Probably nothing. It was just Mr. Corrigan.

ORDERLY. *(As he picks up some of KEVIN'S flowers on the TV.)* He's always getting me into trouble. Last month he put creamed corn in my lab coat pockets. *(Still picking up here and there.)* I'd talk to him about it, but I can never figure out what he's saying.

MONTCRIEF. I don't think you'll have to worry about Mr. Corrigan anymore. *(pause)*

ORDERLY. You still sound mad at me.

MONTCRIEF. It's not you—it, it was a bad night.

ORDERLY. I heard. You going off shift? *(She nods.)* I'm just coming on. *(pause)* We could eat dinner. *(Pause. He gives her one of JULIA'S flowers. She smiles a little.)*

MONTCRIEF. Okay. *(He smiles.)*

ORDERLY. *(as they exit)* Meet me here at six.

(They are gone. Pause. RAYMOND comes in the room, with sheets and starts making the bed. After a few moments, SUTTON enters.)

SUTTON. What are you doing?

RAYMOND. Oh, somebody was down here, asking about Mrs. Muir, and when I got in here I noticed that nobody had given her bed fresh linen. So I did it.

SUTTON. Somebody? Who?

RAYMOND. I don't remember his name.

SUTTON. Kevin somebody?

RAYMOND. Oh no, not him. Some guy from upstairs asking about her room change request. I said, "I don't think she'll be wanting one, now." Where's Mr. Corrigan? Isn't he due out of therapy? *(SUTTON sticks her head out the doorway.)*

SUTTON. *(calling)* Mr. Corrigan? You still down there?

RAYMOND. Sure takes him long enough to get down the hallway.

SUTTON. Well, I'm sorry, but some asshole put him on sedatives and he doesn't move as fast as he used to.

RAYMOND. Touchy, aren't we?

SUTTON. *(as JACK approaches) We* are, yes. *(to JACK)* I'm sorry about that, Mr. C, I got distracted and though you were right behind me. *(HE does not respond, but sits flaccidly in the wheel chair, eyeing RAYMOND. SUTTON clears her throat.)*

RAYMOND. *(Moving to the door, mock cheer.)* Yes, I know the routine— *(Stops at the door.)* Have a nice day, you two.

SUTTON. Thank you. *(RAYMOND leaves.)* Bitch. *(She turns to JACK, who is already wheeling toward his bed.)* How was physical therapy today?

JACK. *(dully)* Fine. *(HE gets in to bed.)*

SUTTON. I have to give you another valium. *(He gives her a low, nasty look.)* Don't give me that look, Mr. C, I only do this because I have to. Now, please make this easy and take the pill—I don't want to give you an injection. *(HE puts out his hand and she gives him the pill. HE puts it in his mouth while SHE pours him some water, and HE drinks the water and gives her back the cup.)* Thanks. *(SHE throws the cup away as HE lies back in bed. SHE starts to say something, thinks better of it. Starts out.)* If you need anything...well...I have to go down to records and fill out some forms, so just don't buzz anyone for an hour, okay? Unless you want Raymond, okay? *(HE doesn't acknowledge her.)* You got your remote—? *(HE picks up the remote control and turns on the TV.)* —control. You do. Good. Alright, I'll see you later.

(SHE leaves. JACK opens his mouth, and sticks out his tongue, which still holds the pill. He takes it off his tongue, looks at it, then places it on his tray, grinding it into powder with a water pitcher. He then methodically sweeps the powdered pill into his hand, and joylessly blows the dust over the room to remove any traces. He brushes off his hands, and sits flaccidly watching TV for a moment before an umbrella bursts through the door. It is followed by KEVIN, in high spirits.)

KEVIN. Hey! Surprise! *(He waits for a response, either from the door or JACK. He folds up the umbrella.)* Don't mean to seem paranoid, but I know what it's like to come in on an off-day. How are you, Jack? Back so soon?

JACK. ...shit.

KEVIN. *(joyously)* Oh, effervescent as always, I see. Where's Julia? I know it's only Wednesday, but something *great* happened yesterday and I promised to keep her posted. *(Holds up the umbrella.)* You think this was funny? *(no response)* So did I. Julia won't, though, you wait. Sure is good to know it warmed your heart, though. *(no response)* Oh, come on, Jack. I didn't think valium made you stupid.

JACK. *(without enthusiasm)* Fuck you.

KEVIN. Thank you, I'm fine. In fact, that's why I'm here today. *(points to the TV)* Maybe you don't watch elections on that thing, but they *do* vote on dreary little things like millages, and our millage *passed! (no response)* Now, calm down, I haven't gotten to the *good* part—that means yours truly has his job back for the next two years! *(pause)* Isn't that great? *(pause)* This would work better with Julia, is she in the Solarium?

JACK. She's dead. *(KEVIN laughs.)*

KEVIN. Well, pack her in ice and get her out here—I got good news. *(Laughs again, no response.)* Come on. *(pause)* I assume she's in the Solarium, since she's not here—

JACK. She's dead, kid. *(pause)*

KEVIN. How stupid do you think I am, Jack? I *see* through all your bullshit, and you're going to give me a civil answer. *(pause)* Okay—I'm sorry. I *did* try to move Julia. I misread the situation completely. I...just don't know you very well, and what little I know I don't like. But...maybe you *are* someone worthwhile. *(JACK laughs soundlessly.)*

JACK. She put you up to this.

KEVIN. No. That's why I wanted to talk to you alone.

JACK. But the words are hers. If I close my eyes, I can almost see her say them.

KEVIN. We think alike. *(Pause. JACK looks at him.)* Okay, the words may be hers—hell, the idea is hers. I'm not going to pretend I like you. *(pause)* This...gesture—this apology...is mine. Can you accept that?

JACK. It doesn't matter.

KEVIN. It matters to me.

JACK. *(coldly)* You don't matter. *(Pause. KEVIN gathers up his flowers and prepares to leave.)*

KEVIN. Yes, I do. And fuck you if you don't know it. Just tell me where she is.

JACK. She's dead.

KEVIN. *(viciously)* Alright, cut that shit out right now! You can like me, or hate me, Jack, I don't care! I'm here for Julia and I'm here for the duration—now where is she?

JACK. *(exploding)* What do you *want* out of me, kid?! How many times are you going to make me say it?! Julia Jane Muir is dead! She's *dead!* Do you want to hear it slower, do you want to hear it louder? Do I have to cough up blood before you believe me? Look at her things! *(Storms over to her bed.)* Do you see her things? They took away her shoes and her clothes, and that miserable fucking music box that used to keep me up nights! They took all of them away! Do you see her chart, or her robe? *(Viciously ripping her bedding up.)* They even took away her bedding so it doesn't smell like her anymore! Miserable fucking antiseptic...

KEVIN. ...how?

JACK. Oh, you want to wallow in it, don't you? You looking for a sentimental ending? Well, no such luck. Bodies aren't sentimental, they just shut down. And hers shut down in her precious useless Solarium... *(laugh)* They didn't even notice until the next morning, they thought she was asleep. Her and that fucking window. Stupid, stupid woman...

KEVIN. *(crossing to the window)* Oh God, I must have been the last to see her alive...

JACK. Do me a favor and emote somewhere else. *(no response)* Hey, get out! *(KEVIN slumps in a chair, burying his head in his hands. JACK crosses over, rips his hands down.)* No, you *look!* This is what life is, kid. When you play the pied piper for the likes of us, you've got to get used to the high turnover rate. Pretty ugly right now, isn't it? But you'll forget how this feels, you'll move on. I'm sure you have someone else waiting for one of your grand gestures—

KEVIN. *(fiercely)* It's not a damned gesture! I wanted it to be—to be something just for *her,* but I wouldn't feel so *rotten* if it was just a gesture! *(HE walks away from JACK, crying. JACK watches him a moment.)*

JACK. *(Crossing to his bed.)* Well, I'm not going to be your Mommy. Don't expect me to step into the void, kid. You're going to learn that the whole world doesn't open up to you just because you can cry. Big deal. The rest of the world cries. The rest of the world gets shit on, too. And they cry... *(angrily)* But the rest of the world doesn't have someone like her! They cry alone...and scream and kick and it doesn't change a damn thing. ...but it's something. Even if you're alone...it's something.

KEVIN. Someone to scream to...

JACK. *(dully)* What?

KEVIN. Nothing...what will you do?

JACK. What do you care?

KEVIN. They'll move someone else in here...I bet you'll raise a fuss.

JACK. So what.

KEVIN. She's a tough act to follow...when is the funeral?

JACK. I don't know. Ask a nurse.

KEVIN. Aren't you going?

JACK. And do what? Just leave, alright?

KEVIN. They can't keep you away as a disciplinary thing.

JACK. Just—leave. I don't know what's happening. I don't care what's happening. I don't care what's happening. That's the last line of defense, kid. Then they can do anything and it won't hurt, because it never matters anyway.

KEVIN. That sounds like a good way to die.

JACK. That's exactly right. But it's *my* way.

KEVIN. *(gesturing outside)* If you give up, you let them win. *(no response)* I never figured you for a coward.

JACK. Well, I am. *(turns on TV)* Now leave me alone. *(pause)* You want me to give you speeches?! I got nothing to say anymore. *(to himself, quoting Butler)* "Oaths are but words, and words but wind..." Goodbye. *(KEVIN leaves, silently. Pause. KEVIN comes back.)*

KEVIN. Who said that?

JACK. Oh, fuck. Will you go?

KEVIN. It wasn't Emerson—

JACK. Get out of here!

KEVIN. Was it Emerson?

JACK. Who cares!

KEVIN. You don't know!

JACK. *(angrily)* Yes, I do—it was Samuel Butler! *(pause)*

KEVIN. Oh. *(starts to leave, starts back)* You want to know what Emerson said?

JACK. *(bellowing)* Go away! *(pause)*

KEVIN. Well, I imagine he said that, too. Want to know what he said about words? *(JACK watches TV. KEVIN crosses to the TV.)* "Words and deeds are quite indifferent modes of the same energy. Words are also action, and actions are a kind of words." *(He turns off the TV.)* Thought you might like to know that next time you feel like screaming.

JACK. Like now?

KEVIN. If you want to. *(pointing)* Your color's better—

JACK. FUCK YOU!

KEVIN. You're welcome. *(Picks up umbrella, starts to go.)* Okay, this is better—see you next week—

JACK. WHAT? Get back here, hard-on. What did you say?

KEVIN. See you next week. Is Thursday okay, or do you want me to take you to the funeral?

JACK. Why are you coming back? *(KEVIN tosses him JULIA'S flowers.)*

KEVIN. To see you, of course.

JACK. *(knocking the flowers all over)* Why?

KEVIN. Why not? You have appointments?

JACK. Don't think—I—! I'm not going—I'm not your Julia, kid! *(Throws some flowers at his feet.)*

KEVIN. I know you're not. You're shorter. And you're male.

JACK. I don't want you back!

KEVIN. And you miss her. That's one thing we have in common.

JACK. Look, I don't like you! And I'll *never* like you!

KEVIN. That's *two* things we have in common. I'm going to see about her funeral. Be back on Thursday.

JACK. Wait! You're not going to show up here.

KEVIN. Watch me.

JACK. I'll block the door! *(getting up)* I'll jam chairs in front of it and I won't let you in! Or worse! WORSE! *(with a maniacal glee)* I can get bed pans, kiddo. I'll drop huge pots of my own shit on your miserable pointed head while I laugh my ass off across the room!

KEVIN. And that'll be the healthiest thing you've done in the last two days. See you Thursday...

JACK. You don't believe me!

KEVIN. Yes, I do.

JACK. Either you don't believe me, or you're not coming back!

KEVIN. *(Crosses to the foot of JACK'S bed, picks up the urinal, tosses it to JACK. Then he grabs his umbrella and opens it.)* Try me, asshole! *(exits)*

JACK. *(yelling after him)* You think you're smart, but you're not, kid! I damn well better not see your lousy fucking face around here ever again! *(From behind the closed door, we hear RAYMOND'S voice.)*

RAYMOND. *(off)* Mr. Corrigan, I won't have this! Now, I know how much you don't like me in there, but if you start acting up again, I'll be in there like a shot—I promise you! *(JACK scowls at the sound of her voice, and then notices he's still holding the urinal. A pleasant thought.)* You've been awful good the last few days... *(JACK crosses to his food tray and, during the following, stuffs his dinner into the urinal.)* I think you've learned that we can cooperate if we all do our part, isn't that so? Mr. Corrigan?

JACK. I'm more than willing to do my part.

RAYMOND. *(still off)* Because, if we don't, we can always

go back to the yelling and screaming. *(JACK smiles, maliciously.)* Now I don't want to hear a PEEP out of you for the next hour, understand?

JACK. Oh, yes.

RAYMOND. *(off)* Good. *(JACK goes to the door, grabs a chair, and hangs the urinal on the sprinkler pipe as before. He crosses toward JULIA'S bed to ring the buzzer, and catches something underfoot. He winces, stops, pulls up one of her flowers. By reflex:)* Julia, god— *(He realizes, stops. Pause. He moves to her bed, sits on it, sniffs the flower and reverently places it on the bed. He smiles at it. With the other hand, he reaches for the call-bell. He pushes the buzzer down, hard. The buzz outside is faintly audible. LIGHTS START to FADE as we hear footsteps approaching. With low joy.)* Peeep.

CURTAIN

PROPERTY PLOT

THE SOLARIUM—

Magazine rack
Various magazines (incl. *National Geographic)*
Bulletin board (w/notices)
Ashtrays

JACK AND JULIA'S ROOM—

JACK'S SIDE:
Cork board w/clippings
Name plate
Buzzer
Clock on nighttable
Lighter
Urinal (hooked on foot of bed)
Remote control (pre-set in bed)
Kleenex package (pre-set in night table)
Shoe box (preset under bed)
Cane
1 robe (on coatrack)
1 robe (w/bladderbag, on coatrack)
Gates (on bed)
Straps (on bed)
Crank (at foot of bed)
Hook for urinal (at foot of bed)
Chart (hooked on nighttable)
Moveable table for food trays
Half-eaten food and tray (for SUTTON to remove in Act I, Sc. 2)
Pitcher for water (on nighttable)
Plastic cups (on table)
Slippers (pre-set under bed)

JULIA'S SIDE:

Cork board w/clippings (must be easily removable for ORDERLY in Act 2)
Nameplate (removable)
Buzzer
Quilt (on bed)
Several dresses (in closet)
Picture
Pitcher for water (later used as vase)
Plastic cups
Moveable table for food trays
Gates (on bed)
Straps (on bed)
Robe (on coatrack)
Slippers (under bed)
Chart (on nighttable)
Various small knick-knacks and figurines (on nighttable)

COMMON AREAS:

Coatrack
Doylie on television
Lace tablecloth on big table
Dancer figurine on musicbox (on big table)
JULIA'S brush and comb set (on big table)
Picture (framed)
Number "412" (on outside of door)
"Conserve Energy" notices on wall (near light-switches)

PERSONAL PROPS

MONTCRIEF

Chart (1/3)
Several charts (2/4)
Pens

KEVIN

Eyeglasses
Watch
3 different sets of flowers
Box of candy (wrapped w/ribbon)
Wallet (2/4)
Umbrella (2/5)

JULIA

Purse
KEVIN'S flowers
Pitcher
Plastic cup
Pillow (1/1)

JACK

Wheelchair (2/2)
Extra cigarettes

SUTTON

Wheelchair (1/2)
Pens
Blood pressure sleeve
Stethoscope
2 pills
Wheelchair (2/5)

RAYMOND

Pens
Stethoscope
Towel (2/1)
KEVIN'S dry clothes (2/1)
Coat (2/4)

ORDERLY

Mop
Bucket
Wringer (on bucket)
Various rags and towels
Tray of food (1/3)
Basket or suitcase for JULIA'S things (2/5)

FURNITURE LIST

THE SOLARIUM

Sofa
2 endtables
Chair
Small table
Lamp
Door unit
Light switch

JACK AND JULIA'S ROOM

Television
Two hospital beds (with mattress cranks)
Door unit (with sprinkler pipe)
Small table
Chair
Night tables for both beds
Porcelain dancer figurine for table
Buzzers on both night tables
2 small clothes closets
Bathroom door unit
Guard rails on walls

HALLWAY (Optional)

Guard rails

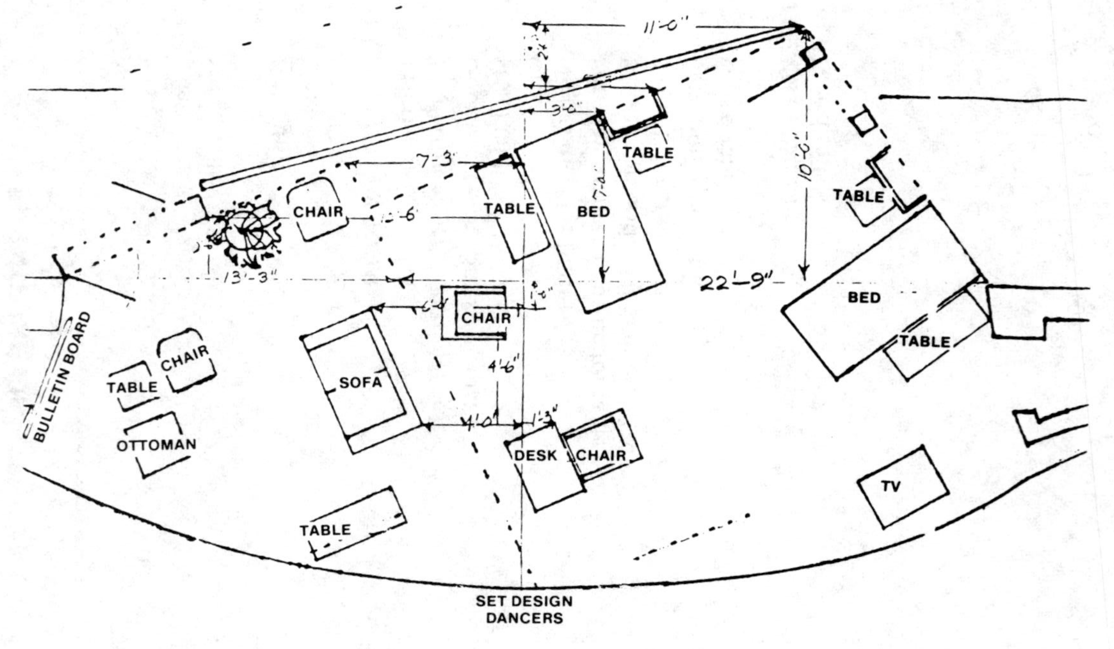

SET DESIGN
DANCERS

Other Publications for Your Interest

BENEFACTORS

(LITTLE THEATRE—COMIC DRAMA)

By MICHAEL FRAYN

2 men, 2 women—Interior

Do not expect another *Noises Off*; here the multi-talented Mr. Frayn has more on his mind than Just Plain Fun. *Benefactors*, a long-running Broadway and London hit, is about doing good and do-gooding (not the same) and about the way the world changes outside your control just when you are trying to change it yourself. The story concerns an architect who has the sixties notion that if you give people good environments they will be good people. But, given a South London development to design, he is forced by town planners to go for a high-rise, characterless scheme. No sooner does he begin to believe in this scheme than the fashion for high rises goes bust. ". . . one of the subtlest plays Broadway has seen in years, by one of the most extraordinary writers of the English-speaking theater . . . more political than most political plays, more intimate than most intimate plays and wiser than almost any play around today."—Newsweek. ". . . a fine . . . very good play . . . A Christmas present for theatergoers."—WABC-TV. ". . . a high point of the theater season . . . rare wit and intelligence."—Wall Street Journal. ". . . fascinating and astonishing play . . ."—N.Y. Daily News. ". . . dazzling and devastating play . . ."—N.Y. Times. ". . . a tour de force . . . simultaneously compelling and alienating . . ."—Christian Science Monitor. (#3980)

PACK OF LIES

(LITTLE THEATRE—DRAMA)

By HUGH WHITEMORE

3 men, 5 women—Combination interior

Bob and Barbara Jackson are a nice middle-aged English couple. Their best friends are their neighbors, Helen and Peter Kroger, who are Canadian. All is blissful in the protected, contained little world of the Jacksons; until, that is, a detective from Scotland Yard asks if his organization may use the Jackson's house as an observation station to try and foil a Soviet spy ring operating in the area. Being Good Citizens the Jacksons oblige, though they become progressively more and more put out as Scotland Yard's demands on them increase. They are really put to the test when the detective reveals to them that the spies are, in fact, their best friends the Krogers. Scotland Yard asks the Jacksons to cooperate with them to trap the spies, which really puts the Jacksons on the horns of a dilemma. Do they have the right to "betray" their friends? "This is a play about the morality of lying, not the theatrics of espionage, and, in Mr. Whitemore's view, lying is a virulent disease that saps patriots and traitors alike of their humanity."—N.Y. Times. "A crackling melodrama."—Wall St. Journal. "Absolutely engrossing . . . an evening of dynamic theatre."—N.Y. Post. "A superior British drama."—Chr. Sci. Mon. (#18154)

Other Publications for Your Interest

THE CURATE SHAKESPEARE AS YOU LIKE IT

(LITTLE THEATRE—COMEDY)

By DON NIGRO

4 men, 3 women—Bare stage

This extremely unusual and original piece is subtitled: "The record of one company's attempt to perform the play by William Shakespeare". When the very prolific Mr. Nigro was asked by a professional theatre company to adapt *As You Like It* so that it could be performed by a company of seven he, of course, came up with a completely original play about a rag-tag group of players comprised of only seven actors led by a dotty old curate who nonetheless must present Shakespeare's play; and the dramatic interest, as well as the comedy, is in their hilarious attempts to impersonate all of Shakespeare's multitude of characters. The play has had numerous productions nationwide, all of which have come about through word of mouth. We are very pleased to make this "underground comic classic" widely available to theatre groups who like their comedy wide open and theatrical. (#5742)

SEASCAPE WITH SHARKS AND DANCER

(LITTLE THEATRE—DRAMA)

By DON NIGRO

1 man, 1 woman—Interior

This is a fine new play by an author of great talent and promise. We are very glad to be introducing Mr. Nigro's work to a wide audience with *Seascape With Sharks and Dancer*, which comes directly from a sold-out, critically acclaimed production at the world-famous Oregon Shakespeare Festival. The play is set in a beach bungalow. The young man who lives there has pulled a lost young woman from the ocean. Soon, she finds herself trapped in his life and torn between her need to come to rest somewhere and her certainty that all human relationships turn eventually into nightmares. The struggle between his tolerant and gently ironic approach to life and her strategy of suspicion and attack becomes a kind of war about love and creation which neither can afford to lose. In other words, this is quite an offbeat, wonderful love story. We would like to point out that the play also contains a wealth of excellent ***monologue*** and ***scene material.*** (#21060)

Other Publications for Your Interest

THE BALLAD OF SOAPY SMITH

(ADVANCED GROUPS—EPIC COMIC DRAMA)

By MICHAEL WELLER

24 men, 9 women (with doubling)—Various interiors and exteriors (may be unit set)

"Col." Jefferson Randolph Smith, known as "Soapy" to his friends and foes, is a celebrated, notorious con man whose reputation has, alas, not preceded him to the Alaska Gold Rush town of Skagway in 1897, when the play takes place. Soapy is a charming gentleman, and he starts up a protection racket which brings law and order to the town, giving it a church and an infirmary. Oddly enough Soapy, the criminal, becomes a force for moral good; until the town's hypocrisy and vicious self interest bring him down, a victim of the cardinal sin of believing in his own con. "Michael Weller deserves praise for a historical play with contemporary relevance, daring to accost a large canvas. The protagonist is a complex and absorbing creation. I left the theatre, for once, thinking rather than trying to forget."—N.Y. Mag. "A rousing epic"—AP. "A good time on a grand scale, with a mind and vision of rare intensity."—Gannett/Westchester Newsp. **(#3975)**

HURLYBURLY

(ADVANCED GROUPS—DRAMA)

By DAVID RABE

4 men, 3 women—Interior

This rivetting new drama by the author of *The Basic Training of Pavlo Hummel*, *Sticks and Bones* and *Streamers* took New York by storm in a production directed by Mike Nichols and starring William Hurt, Sigourney Weaver, Judith Ivey, Christopher Walken, Harvey Keitel and Jerry Stiller. Quite a cast, and quite a play! The drama is the story of four men nosedeep in the decadent, perverted, cocaine-laden culture that is Hollywood; pursuing their sex-crazed, dope-ridden vision of the American Dream. "*Hurlyburly* offers some of Mr. Rabe's most inventive and disturbing writing. At his impressive best, Mr. Rabe makes grim, ribald and surprisingly compassionate comedy out of the lies and rationalizations that allow his alienated men to keep functioning (if not feeling) in the fogs of lotusland. They work in an industry so corrupt that its only honest executives are those who openly admit that they lie."—N.Y. Times. "Rabe has written a strange, bitterly funny, self-indulgent, important play."—N.Y. Post. "An important work, masterly accomplished."—Time. "A powerful permanent contribution to American drama . . . rivetting, disturbing, fearsomely funny . . . has a savage sincerity and a crackling theatrical vitality. This deeply felt play deserves as wide an audience as possible."—Newsweek. (#10163)

Other Publications for Your Interest

THE OCTETTE BRIDGE CLUB

(LITTLE THEATRE—COMIC DRAMA)

By P.J. BARRY

1 man, 8 women—Interior

There are no less than *eight wonderful roles for women* in this delightful sentimental comedy about American life in the 30's and 40's. On alternate Friday evenings, eight sisters meet to play bridge, gossip and generally entertain themselves. They are a group portrait right out of Norman Rockwell America. The first act takes place in 1934; the second act, ten years later, during a Hallowe'en costume/bridge party. Each sister acts out her character, climaxing with the youngest sister's hilarious belly dance as Salome. She, whom we have perceived in the first act as being somewhat emotionally distraught, has just gotten out of a sanitarium, and has realized that she must cut the bonds that have tied her to her smothering family and strike out on her own. This wonderful look at an American family in an era far more innocent and naive than our own was quite a standout at the Actors Theatre of Louisville Humana Festival of New American Plays. The play did not succeed with Broadway's jaded critics (which these days just may be a mark in its favor); but we truly believe it is a perfect play for Everybody Else; particularly, community theatres with hordes of good actresses clamoring for roles. "One of the most charming plays to come to the stage this season . . . a delightful, funny, moving glimpse of the sort of lives we are all familiar with—our own."—NY Daily News "Counterpunch". (#17056)

BIG MAGGIE

(LITTLE THEATRE—DRAMA)

By JOHN B. KEANE

5 men, 6 women—Exterior/Interior

We are very proud to be making available for U.S. production the most popular play by one of contemporary Ireland's most beloved playwrights. The title character is the domineering mother of four wayward, grown-up children, each determined to go his own way, as Youth will do—and each likely headed in the wrong direction. Maggie has been burdened with a bibulous, womanizing husband. Now that he has died, though, she is free to exercise some control over the lives of herself and her family, much to the consternation of her children. Wonderful character parts abound in this tightly-constructed audience-pleaser, none finer than the role of Maggie—a gem of a part for a middle-aged actress! "The feminist awareness that informs the play gives it an intriguing texture, as we watch it unfold against a colorfully detailed background of contemporary rural Ireland. It is at times like hearing Ibsen with an Irish brogue."—WWD. (#4637)